A
PRACTICAL
WEDDING

A

PRACTICAL
WEDDING

CREATIVE IDEAS *for* PLANNING *a* BEAUTIFUL,
AFFORDABLE, *and* MEANINGFUL CELEBRATION

MEG KEENE

Da Capo
LIFE
LONG

A Member of the Perseus Books Group

Printed in the United States of America. For information, address Da Capo Press, 44 Farnsworth Street, 3rd Floor, Boston, MA 02210.

Library of Congress Cataloging-in-Publication Data
Keene, Meg.
    A practical wedding : creative solutions for planning a beautiful, affordable, and meaningful celebration / Meg Keene.—1st ed.
        p.   cm.
    Includes index.
    ISBN 978-0-7382-1515-0 (pbk. : alk. paper)—ISBN 978-0-7382-1545-7 (e-book)
    1. Weddings—Economic aspects. I. Title.
    HQ745.K44 2012
    395.2'2—dc23

                                                                    2011035205

First Da Capo Press edition 2012

Published by Da Capo Press
A Member of the Perseus Books Group
www.dacapopress.com

Da Capo Press books are available at special discounts for bulk purchases in the US by corporations, institutions, and other organizations. For more information, please contact the Special Markets Department at the Perseus Books Group, 2300 Chestnut Street, Suite 200, Philadelphia, PA, 19103, or call (800) 810-4145, ext. 5000, or e-mail special.markets@perseusbooks.com.

10 9 8

The wedding was very much like other weddings, where the parties have no taste for finery or parade; and Mrs. Elton, from the particulars detailed by her husband, thought it all extremely shabby, and very inferior to her own. "Very little white satin, very few lace veils; a most pitiful business!" . . . But, in spite of these deficiencies, the wishes, the hopes, the confidence, the predictions, of the small band of true friends who witnessed the ceremony, were fully answered in the perfect happiness of the union.

—Jane Austen, *Emma*

Getting married is an attempt at turning air into matter, transforming the ineffable workings of the heart into things that are "real": the invitation, the dress, the ring. The words that constitute a wedding are magical incantations of the highest order. In the presence of witnesses and voiced by a vested authority, two people are pronounced a single unit. Ta-da!

—Anita Diamant, *Pitching My Tent*

You get to a point where there's not much you can do but put on your fancy party dress and a pair of fabulous shoes and grab a bottle of cheap champagne to swig with your girls on the way to meet your groom.

—APracticalWedding.com comment

CONTENTS

WHAT
REALLY
MATTERS

*H*ere is what everyone fails to mention before your wedding: Getting married? It's huge. It's bigger than you ever expected or imagined. It's life-changing. And having done it, I can categorically say that it is not about the cute cake, or the glamorous dress, or the luscious flowers (though each of those things can be really fun). It's not even about the beautiful ceremony site or the packed dance floor. It's about something more monumental than all of that. It's about the look on your partner's face as you walk down the aisle. It's about that moment when you exchange rings and somehow transform love into matter. It's about how vowing to care for your partner for the rest of your life, in front of a group of witnesses, subtly changes you. It's about seeing your most unsentimental friends openly cry. It's about the feeling that sweeps over when you fully realize that you have so many people you love in the same room at the same time (or a handful of people you love the most circling you in the courthouse), and that they are all there to celebrate the massive commitment you are making.

A whole industry is set up to sell you a beautiful wedding; it's set up to sell you how things will look. But what matters on your wedding day, what you will remember until you are old and gray, is how it felt. The carefully crafted details are, in the end, just that: details. They barely hit your radar screen on your wedding day. The things that stick with you are those that you could never ever plan. For me it was the four-year-old daughter of our lifelong friend who dressed herself in bright red cowboy boots and an enormous pink hair flower; the wedding dress from the 1950s that I stumbled on in a vintage shop at the last minute; my husband's oldest friend holding my bouquet while I put on my makeup; feeling our lives intertwine as we circled each other under the chuppah; laughing as everyone shared stories.

But as wonderful as the wedding can be, planning it is one of the most complicated and loaded processes of modern adulthood. Getting from newly engaged all the way to your wedding day while staying sane and solvent sometimes feels impossible. The process of negotiating things like faith, money, family, and tradition, all in a very public way, would be difficult in the best of circumstances. When you add the enormous cultural pressures of the modern wedding, you can get something akin to disaster.

I assume that if you are reading this, you are probably engaged. That means you are in one of two places. You're in the first stages of bliss and excitement—whole life together! Wedding to plan! Sparkly new ring (perhaps)! Or you've moved on to stage two—where you realize that planning even a sensible wedding is going to cost two to three times what you expected, and going to take five to ten times the effort that it reasonably should. Oh. And then there are the expectations. The endless, conflicting expectations.

A cursory glance at a wedding magazine or etiquette book will give you an idea of where the expectations are coming from. First of all, there are the lists. Every book or wedding magazine has *lists*—lists ordering that you immediately do *this*, lists forcefully suggesting that maybe you should start doing *that*, mile-long lists of activities that you need to complete if you want to be a Proper Bride. Worse, these books claim to have both etiquette and tradition on their side (they have neither, but we'll come back to that), which ends up making you feel more than a little inadequate and crazy.

The average wedding planning book will talk you through everything you ostensibly need to know, in mind-numbing, illustrated detail. It will talk you through your fabric choices for wedding dresses (which is fascinating until you realize that, although gainfully employed, the only wedding dress material you can actually afford is inexplicably a poorly manufactured polyester— even though you were pretty sure what you needed to have was French lace). It will talk you through what kind of chairs (or chair covers) you need, every flower that you must know before you pick out your centerpieces, and generally all the things that Must Be Done or everyone will be Horribly Offended.

If the expectations ended there, we would be more or less fine. Half insane, but generally fine. Wedding websites can be ignored; charlatans selling monogrammed favors under the guise of etiquette can be scoffed at. But the problem is, expectations run so much deeper than that.

First of all, and most simply, there are our own expectations. After years of seeing weddings with lines of matching bridesmaids, piles of expensive food, and all-night dance parties, most of us have a small outline in our heads of what we want: a silk wedding dress, letterpress invitations, pretty flowers, good food, and a wonderful party. That's not so hard, right? This won't be that expensive, right? Well. If only.

Then there are the expectations of our parents. Our parents want things. They want reasonable things. They want to see us tremendously happy. They want to not be embarrassed when they invite friends, whose children's lavish weddings they have been attending for years. They want to look like a happy and normal family at this, the pinnacle of public family life. The problem is that "normal" and "not embarrassing" in Wedding Land have come to look a lot like a banquet room at the Ritz and a slowly melting ice sculpture . . . that, and a giant wad of cash you no longer have.

And finally there is Everyone Else. Unless you have thrown a wedding or had a baby, you have not met Everyone Else. All those neighbors and coworkers and people at the post office? Before, they were just people we saw sometimes. Now they are our Greek chorus. "Let me see the ring! Ooooohhh, it's big! You must be thrilled!" "How many bridesmaids are you having and what are they wearing?" "What are your colors? You have to have colors!" "Now, try not to spend a down payment on the wedding dress, little lady, no matter how much you want to." "Aren't grooms the worst? They just can't help out to save their lives!"

The problem with expectations is not the sentiment behind them. People genuinely love weddings, want to see you happy, and want to *chat* with you about it (God bless them). The problem is when expectations slowly strip you of your capacity to do anything other than what is prescribed. And what is pre-scribed tends to be massively expensive and stressful enough to give you a need for mood-altering drugs or a hankering for a nightly whiskey.

But here is the kicker: everything we're being sold as What We Need to Do for Tradition's Sake has little or nothing to do with the kinds of weddings our grandmothers had or, more dramatically, that our great-great-grandmothers had. One hundred and fifty years ago, most Americans were still getting married at home, in their parlor, in their best dresses, holding a prayer book or an embroidered handkerchief. One hundred years ago, most weddings had moved to the church, with only some brides wearing white, and the union was often celebrated by a tea party or a wedding breakfast. As for our grandmothers' era? Well, my grandmother took a taxi from Alabama to California at the end of World War II, since the trains were not running for civilians, and got married as soon as my grandfather was released from a Japanese prisoner-of-war camp. She wore the one white satin dress she could find in the store, and her attendants were the nurses from the naval hospital where my grandfather was being treated. Other than the white dress, the cake, the flowers, the vows, and the ring, there is next to nothing in modern wedding traditions that my grandmother would recognize, let alone approve of.

How do we plan a modern wedding while keeping our souls and our sanity intact? I suggest that we do so thoughtfully, and carefully, with an eye both to actual history and tradition, as well as to our relationships. In the past twenty years, weddings have become shockingly homogenized. The list of musts has grown longer and longer, threatening to take both the couple and their finances down with it. If we scale back to the level of formality and expense that our grandmothers and great-grandmothers would approve of, and then add and subtract from there, we might make it through alive, and we will have a better chance of remembering what this party is about. That, and we'll have the ironclad justifications of actual history, and actual tradition, on our side.

1

GETTING
STARTED

Here We Go . . .

You've just gotten engaged! You're thrilled, your parents are thrilled, and your friends are giddy for you. So what should you do next? Well, nothing. Nothing except tipsily sip champagne and passionately kiss your partner. Take some time, and enjoy being engaged. Celebrate.

When people start asking you about the wedding, tell them, "Oh goodness, we're just so excited to be engaged, we haven't even thought about that yet." Then, when you've spent at least two weeks enjoying the feeling of glee and bliss, you're ready to start the planning process . . . slowly.

In this chapter, I'll walk you through the first steps: finding your way through the process of being newly engaged, dreaming up ideas for your wedding, and then slowly aligning those dreams with reality (without losing any of the joy). If you learn nothing else from wedding planning, my wish is that you learn to say yes

A PRACTICAL BRIDE SPEAKS

Finding Wedding Zen
BY ALYSSA MOONEY

I am not the bride you need to emulate; I'm the one you should learn from. I was bound and determined to have a stress-free wedding—so bound and determined that I worked myself into a tizzy trying to not stress over the wedding. You know the stereotypical bride who carries around eighteen wedding magazines and a binder full of business cards and idea pages? I was the modern indie version, with a favorites folder full of blogs and idea websites, pictures from Flickr that had color combos I loved, and my own inspiration board in PowerPoint because I couldn't convince my future husband that I absolutely, positively needed Photoshop (Lord knows I tried). I think my biggest regret is that in trying so hard to not be That Bride, I nearly ended up being That Bride. And That Bride is not pretty.

So here's my wedding wisdom: find your Wedding Zen. It's that middle ground between caring enough to make something happen but not giving a damn if it doesn't. It's like Shangri-la: hard to find but a beautiful place to be.

Figure out what you care about—I mean, what you really care about. Because trust me, once you start getting caught up in planning mode, you'll start caring about things you never thought you would. Also realize that some of the things you think will be the easiest will become some of the hardest. It's just going to happen. My thing was my

[continues]

to what makes you happy, and a kind but firm no to things that are wrong for you. And if you can remember during this whole planning process that all you really need is the man, the preacher, and the dress (or the woman, the officiant, and the stylish pantsuit)? Well, you'll be halfway to Wedding Zen already.

shoes. I thought, "Oh, I can find cream-colored flats anywhere. That won't be a problem." Sounds like an easy thing . . . and then I ended up spray-painting a pair of zebra-print flats two days before the wedding. Know how hard it is to spray-paint shoes, especially when you're crying and furious at yourself for crying? Not my proudest moment.

But luckily, somewhere in there, I found my Wedding Zen. Actually, I can tell you exactly when it was: about noon on the day before my wedding, after I'd been up very late trying to finish my DIY projects. I was alone in my apartment and suddenly it hit me. . . . Holy hell. I was getting married! All the stress just fell away and I started getting excited. I popped open a bottle of champagne intended for the wedding and said, *Screw it. I'm getting married and it's going to be awesome.* I really wish I could tell you how to achieve this Wedding Zen, but I think it just comes when you've done all you can to make things go right and then the wedding angels look down on you and say, "Poor baby, you need to calm it down." And then you do, because you realize that what Grammy kept telling you really is true.

All you need is the man, the preacher, and the dress.

Or the man, the justice of the peace, and the stylish pantsuit.

Or the woman, the officiant, and two dresses.

Or whatever. But that really is all you need.

You may want the other stuff, and it may be awesome when you get that other stuff, or hilarious when that other stuff goes horribly awry, but when it comes down to it, you only need to have what you really need. Which is him or her, and someone to make it official in your hearts.

And the outfit. Because the outfit is important. It is your day to be a pretty princess, damn it.

Joy: Yes, It's Fundamental

I know what you're thinking: Joy? This is the first subject in a
wedding planning handbook? Yes, my friends, it is. Because joy,
full-throated, fully present, vibrating joy like you've never felt?
That is what your wedding is about. That is the "why" in this
planning process, and that is always, always the goal.

Though our wedding day wasn't the best day of my life (nor
was it perfect), it was one of the great joys of my life. When I
showed up on my wedding day, I made the conscious decision
to let everything go and just be as present as I could be (we'll
discuss how to actually pull this off in Chapter 9). In almost
every single wedding picture, I'm grinning my head off. Britta
Nielsen, who married on family property in Washington, described her wedding this way: "There was dancing and 'Bo-
hemian Rhapsody' and fireworks. I saw nothing but grins in
every direction. I'd be hard-pressed to think of a happier day."
When you look back at your wedding, you'll want to remember
how happy you both were. You won't care too much about how
the details looked; you'll care about how you felt. So it's important
to focus your planning on things that will make you a nonstop-
grinning ball of happiness.

And yet somehow, in the world of weddings, very little ink is
spilled on joy. We see a lot of pictures of the bride looking beautiful and of the decorations looking quirky and artful, but very few
pictures that show the bride and groom, heads thrown back, grinning, eyes twinkling with delight. Anna Plumb, who married her
scientist husband outside of a rock and minerals museum near
Portland, Oregon, told me, "Before we got married I thought
that I would sob my eyes out during the ceremony, but mostly I
laughed. Almost all of our photos show my mouth wide open in
laughter or the two of us grinning like idiots at each other." While
it's impossible to know if you'll laugh or cry during your ceremony,

The Proposal

The diamond industry has pulled a fast one over on us. It has convinced us that there is no way to make public a lifetime commitment to another person without a very large, sparkly rock on a very slim band. This is, of course, nonsense.

Often wedding books have engagement chapters that read like diamond-buying guides. But the truth is, the way to get engaged is for the two of you to decide that you want to get married. So the next time someone tries to imply that you are not engaged because you don't have a dramatic enough engagement story or a ring, firmly say, "You know, I like to think of my partner as my rock," and slowly raise your eyebrow.

The modern wedding industry—along with a fair share of romantic comedies—has set a pretty high bar for proposals. We think they need to be elaborate and surprising. But they don't. A proposal should be:

- A decision to get married
- Romantic (because you decide to spend the rest of your lives together, not necessarily because of its elaborate nature)
- Possibly mutual
- Possibly discussed in advance
- Possibly instigated by you
- Not used to judge the state of your relationship
- An event that may be followed by the not-at-all-romantic kind of sobbing, because you realize your life is changing forever

It's exciting to decide to get married. And scary. But the moment of proposal is just that: a moment. It moves you to the next step of the process; it's not the be-all, end-all. So maybe you have a fancy candlelight dinner followed by parachutists delivering you a pear-shaped, seven-carat diamond. Or maybe you decide to get married one Sunday morning over the newspaper and a cup of coffee. Either way is fine. The point is that you decided to spend your life with someone you love.

you should focus your planning on things that make you feel delighted and alive. Because if what you are able to give your guests is yourself in your purest form, if you are able to lead them by joyful and relaxed example, then you are giving them the greatest gift you can give. Your wedding will be one for the history books—not because it was the prettiest party anyone has ever seen, not because you played by all the rules and hit every single mark, but because it was so real, so true, so indescribably full of joy.

Remember what your wedding is: a celebration. It's a reason to rejoice. And it's as simple and as complicated as that.

The Real Purpose of the Engagement

You're about to spend the next few months being feted because you found the right person to settle down with. Chances are, you will have a bunch of parties (engagement party, bachelorette, shower—to be discussed in more detail in Chapter 5), topped off by the one party to rule them all. You will swim in a pile of silk, tulle, balloons, sparkles—and spreadsheets and stress—while you plan your wedding. This can be, by turns, fun and overwhelming, but it is not the purpose of the engagement. The real reason for the engagement is to adjust to the idea of forming a brand-new family unit and making a major life transition. This period is about getting to know your fiancé's family in a different way and to allow you and your family of origin time to work through the inevitable changes.

Oh, and to fight.

The other reason for your engagement is to give you time to yell at one another or to, um, gracefully hash out the big issues. It's better to yell your way through how you will set boundaries with your mother-in-law now than to fight your way through it the week following the wedding after suddenly realizing you don't see eye to eye on this *at all*.

Being engaged is not just about planning a wedding. Yes, you'll want to try on wedding gowns or make the perfect dance mix for your iPod. But this is also a time to focus on your relationship and discuss your shared dreams and goals.

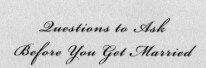

Questions to Ask
Before You Get Married

Though I think everyone walking down the aisle should seek out premarital counseling (whether it's secular or religious in nature), it's also helpful to have tons of in-depth conversations with your partner in the comfort of your own home. With the help of the readers of APracticalWedding.com, I compiled this list of questions to kick off your discussions, which will hopefully last a lifetime.

FAITH
What do we each believe on a personal level?
How do you view spirituality?
Do you pray?
What belief structure do we want in our household?
What does that look like on a theoretical level?
What does that look like day to day?
What holidays will we celebrate and why?

MONEY
What is the exact state of your finances?
What are your assets and liabilities?
How do you want to share finances?
How do you feel about debt?
Is a prenuptial agreement something you want to discuss, for legal or personal reasons? How do we each feel about this issue?
What are your savings/financial goals?
What sort of life do we want to build together, and how much would that cost?

[continues]

Do either of us expect to support our parents at any point in our lives?

GOALS

What sort of careers do we want?

How do we see family fitting in to those careers?

What sort of non-career goals do we have?

What are our fun and frivolous goals?

FAMILY

Do you want kids?

If you don't want kids, why not?

If you do want kids, how many?

What if one of us changes our mind about kids?

What if we are infertile?

What do we expect our parenting styles to be?

How do we expect to share parenting duties?

What do we expect our relationships with our families of origin to look like?

LOCATION

Do we want to live in an urban/suburban/rural environment?

Are there locations that are deal breakers for either of us?

What if one of us got a great job across the country?

How do we feel about living near family?

SEX

How often do you expect to have it?

Do you expect that to change over the years?

Is there anything you like that I don't know about?

Do we expect to be monogamous?

What happens if one of us screws up and sleeps with someone once?

What happens if one of us has an affair?

[continues]

What happens if one of us is unhappy with our sex life?

Would we be willing to visit a sex therapist?

HOUSEHOLD RESPONSIBILITIES

How do we plan to divide up chores and responsibilities?

What happens if one of us isn't pulling our weight in the household?

Does one of us feel like we are in charge of certain tasks, and is that okay with the other person?

Do we have similar standards for cleanliness and life organization?

If we don't have similar standards, are we willing to meet in the middle?

FIGHTING

What's your argument style?

What fighting styles scare you?

What kind of fighting feels okay to you?

How did your parents and loved ones fight, and how does that shape how you fight?

How do we feel about divorce as a potential, if not ideal, outcome to marriage?

What is your personal history with divorce, and how does it shape your view of marriage?

Would you agree to go to couple's counseling with me if I ever requested it?

SKELETONS IN THE CLOSET

Are there any difficult topics that you need to share with me?

Were you physically or sexually abused at any point, or do you suspect that there might be childhood traumas that you don't remember?

Is there anything about past relationships that you need to bring up (emotional or physical abuse, STDs, unresolved emotional issues)?

[continues]

QUESTIONS TO ASK BEFORE YOU GET MARRIED [continued]

Is there a history of physical or mental illness for you or for your
family?

Is there anything I should know about you that I wouldn't know
to ask?

END OF LIFE

What would happen if one of us became unable to care for ourselves over the short or long term?

What sort of end-of-life care does each of us expect?

What do you expect in terms of funeral and burial?

If one of us were to die young, what are our thoughts on
remarriage?

Brainstorming with Your Partner

So, you've relaxed. You've enjoyed being engaged. You've drunk
a lot of celebratory champagne. Maybe you've even started having some long talks about what you want your marriage to be
like. Now you're ready to get started planning!

First let me emphasize: this book is going to be about two
people planning a wedding together. On your wedding day,
there will be two people getting married. And although you
might care more about color combinations than your partner
does, he or she might end up caring more about the music than
you do. And you won't know until you ask. As Lisa Dennis,
who got married in the LDS temple in Bountiful, Utah, said,
"A wedding is not a surprise party for the groom." So it's time to
sit down with your partner and have your first long wedding-
planning talk.

Step One: Crazy, Wild, Wonderful Dreams

The first thing to do is to brainstorm and to dream. Let yourself dream unrestricted by reality at first, because the heart has a way of guiding you in the right direction, even when the heart seems a little crazy. Ask yourself, if you could have any kind of wedding in the world, what would it be? Maybe you want to wear a silk shift as you get married under the Eiffel Tower after you've run away to live in Paris together. That's a pretty fantastic dream—write that down. What are your partner's crazy dreams? Write those down, too.

Once you've come up with your crazy dreams, think about why they make you grin. Maybe you are delighted by the idea of wearing a simple silk dress. Perhaps you really want a tiny wedding outside in a beautiful location. Or maybe it's as simple as wanting to feel like your wedding is the start of a great adventure. Write all of these dreams down. We're going to try to optimize the parts of the wedding that make you happy.

Step Two: Slightly More Pragmatic Details

Now that you've dreamed as crazy and as big as you can, use that information to figure out the type of wedding that you each think you want on a more pragmatic level. Don't worry if you don't agree at this point.

First off, what does each of you think is an ideal wedding size? Do you want a big party with all of your friends and family, or do you want a small ceremony at the courthouse? Ask yourself why. What is it about the wedding you have envisioned in your head that's important? Articulate this. Perhaps you want a big wedding because you have a big family, or maybe you just have a taste for glitz and figure this is one of the few chances you're going to have to throw a black-tie party. If you want a small wedding at the courthouse, maybe you don't like being the center of attention, or maybe you just want something as low-stress as possible. Write all of this down.

Next up, ponder the kind of vibe you'd each like in your wedding. Jen Smith, who had a decidedly counterculture wedding in a hotel ballroom in Northern California, explained, "A wedding can be many things—fun, beautiful, religious, charming, traditional, exciting, quick, quirky, unusual, etc. Trying to plan a wedding that is *all* of those things would drive you insane pretty quickly. We decided that what we wanted was for the wedding to be fun and comfortable." You can't do it all, so figure out what's most important to you. Liz Moorhead, whose reception was in a church social hall in Philadelphia, told me, "Josh and I are atypical traditionalists. I know the indie-chic thing right now is the rustic wedding. But that's so not us. We wanted to channel Audrey Hepburn and Cary Grant at a lavish, jazz-music-pumpin', champagne-flowin', hot-damn party chock-full of garters and bouquet tosses and all the usual wedding junk. So we did. We got married on October 11 at three p.m. Yes, that's a Sunday. Yep, middle of the afternoon. We had a dessert reception." So figure out what your vision is, as a duo. Maybe you want a crazy dance party or a small and elegant dinner party. Or maybe you want a laid-back picnic or a formal afternoon tea. Dreams that initially seem to conflict are okay, too. If you want a low-stress black-tie party, you're probably on to something. You're about to learn that the peculiar magic of weddings is that when you least expect it, they make the impossible possible.

Now, both you and your partner should ask yourselves, "What do we want our wedding to feel like?" Focus your ideal vibe on a feeling. A "champagne-flowin', hot-damn party" gives you a very specific sensation to shoot for; "pretty and purple" does not. Most of what you see focuses on how a wedding looks, so I want you to keep this in mind (stick it on your fridge

Brainstorming Your Wedding Vibe

Perhaps you need a little help brainstorming your wedding vibe. What fun! Here is a list of ideas to get you started. Remember: don't worry about picking words that seem to conflict. You can have a lavish low-budget wedding, or a nontraditional religious wedding. Pick words that you're drawn to, logic be damned.

adventurous	hilarious	relaxed
authentic	inclusive	religious
boozy	informal	reverent
community-oriented	intimate	rustic
	irreverent	sacred
elegant	kid-friendly	sentimental
family-focused	laid-back	simple
freewheeling	lavish	sophisticated
full of laughter	meaningful	thoughtful
full of love	nontraditional	traditional
fun	personal	urban
glamorous	quirky	wild celebration
grown-up	raging dance	pure joy
handcrafted	party	

if you must): "I will not remember what our wedding looked like; I will remember what it felt like."

Step Three: Start Looking at Wedding Inspiration—Cautiously

Once you've had these initial conversations, you're ready to start looking at wedding inspiration. As you start to move into the sometimes-frenzied inspiration phase of wedding planning, be wary! Looking at wedding pictures can start out as insanely fun but can quickly become stressful if you try to figure out how to live up to what you're seeing. The truth is, the pictures you are looking at are not quite real. They've been edited to show you just the best and the prettiest moments of a wedding. Add to that the fact that the wedding pictures you're looking at are often from weddings with, um, quite large budgets, and it might turn out that the flawless backyard wedding you're admiring was actually thrown at a movie star's estate. This might not be totally replicable in your backyard. So once you move past the stage of happily burying yourself in every wedding picture you can find because "I'm getting married, damn it," put on your rational hat. Does that look like a normal backyard wedding? No? Then it's probably not one.

That said, wedding inspiration is ten kinds of fun and can be helpful. What makes you feel tingly when you look at it? Perhaps it's the potluck wedding held in a church rec hall, where everyone looks overjoyed and pie is served instead of wedding cake. Or maybe it's the black-tie reception at one of the colleges at Oxford. Pay attention to that. Wedding pictures can allow you to break out of the box of What Is Always Done at Weddings, and to figure out what your heart desires. Maybe you see a bride in a short dress or in red shoes, and you realize that hey, a long white dress with traditional shoes is not for you. Brilliant! Write down or create a file of things that make you happy.

Step Four: From Ideas to a Tentative Plan

Now you and your partner have a welter of ideas. Boil it down to a few key items. Maybe you want something affordable, low-stress, and fancy. That's great! I know those things sound conflicting, but combining them is still immanently possible. Write down your ideas and put them on your fridge or somewhere you'll see them every day. Wedding planning sometimes takes on a life of its own, and you might suddenly find yourself crying while you call around trying to find a country club to fit your families' two hundred–person guest list. When you can't figure out why you're so sad, you can come back to your stated goal of "small, relaxed, and fun wedding on the beach somewhere," and readjust.

Bringing in the Families

Families Are Complicated

As one of my friends told me at some stressed-out juncture or another during our planning, "There is a reason families don't go on the honeymoon." Oh boy, is that true. By which I mean to say, wedding planning can cause a lot more family stress than we imagine.

For most of our lives, we've absorbed messages from popular culture that weddings are a time to bond with our families and have wonderful, emotional, remember-on-our-deathbed moments with our mothers. The truth is, for most of us, families are loving, messy, complicated creatures. For many families, wedding planning looks nothing like it does in the movies. It involves a lot of hugs and smiles, but also a fair number of arguments and tears. This is normal.

In the modern world, since many couples live together before the wedding, the whole event is often mistaken for a purely symbolic rite of passage. But weddings are more than symbols—they change family dynamics in significant ways. During the wedding planning process, you are moving toward building a new primary family unit, and that can be stressful for everyone concerned. Understand that your wedding and your emerging family unit can be hard on your parents in ways that are difficult for you to grasp. So practice compassion and a real ability to listen.

Know What's Non-Negotiable

Because your wedding will likely be important and emotional for your families, it's valuable to know what's non-negotiable for the two of you when you walk into the first conversation with your parents. Take that list of key ideas that you and your partner came up with, and figure out what you can't budge on. Our list looked a little like this: a big enough wedding that we could invite all our closest friends and family; held in the area where we were living; a Jewish ceremony; and a kick-ass dance party. For us, those items were totally off the table for discussion, which meant that when they came up in conversation with our parents, we *always* presented a united front. Remember that the choices you are making about your wedding are the first choices you are making as a brand-new-baby family, and they are practice for the much bigger choices in your future.

Then? Compromise, Compromise, Compromise

Once you've figured out your non-negotiables, it's time to learn the key word for all weddings (heck, for everything that has to do with family, ever): compromise. Molly Wiedel Till, who got married on top of a mountain in Arizona and held her reception in a traditional social hall, explained how they approached balancing various interests: "For us, staying sane came down to just remembering what mattered to us—the ceremony and having a frackin' amazing dance party—and then remembering what mattered to the people we were spending this best day ever with—traditional stuff like open bars and garter tosses." So sit down with your families, ask what they care about, and really listen. Write it down. Then tell your families that you'll do your very best to balance everyone's needs and that you love them no matter what decisions you end up making.

The wedding day is not your day; it is everyone's day. But this is *your* wedding. So if your mom wants a three hundred–person formal sit-down dinner at the Ritz, and you and your partner want a family-only ceremony at the courthouse, well, maybe you can have a formal sit-down dinner with your family after you go to the courthouse. Try to respect and honor your families' dreams for the wedding, but make sure that first and foremost, your emotional needs are being met.

The Anti To-Do List

Now you've talked with your partner, and you've talked to your families. At this point the two of you should have a pretty clear idea of what you'd like to aim for, if reality doesn't get in the way. Before we get into the nitty-gritty of planning, it's time to take a moment to think of what you don't need to do (because there is so, so much of it).

Print out one of those endless wedding checklists from the Internet, or find one in a magazine. Sit down with a girlfriend who has already gotten married (and has a good head on her shoulders) and a cocktail. Get out a red pen, and circle only the things that are absolutely necessary. By necessary I mean, you should have a list that reads something like this:

- A partner you love (if this wasn't listed on your preprinted list, feel free to write it in nice and big at the top)

- An officiant

- Witnesses

- Something to wear

Then take a green pen and circle the things you actually care about. Not the stuff your wedding self cares about, or the stuff you think you have to care about, or the stuff the list tells you that you have to care about, but the stuff *you* actually care about. Then, next to each item, write *why* you care or *how* you care. Maybe you care about invitations because you majored in studio art in college. Maybe you care about what you're going to eat because you are foodies. Maybe you hate wedding cake, but you really want to cut a wedding blackberry cobbler. Great! Write those things down.

Then take the red pen and cross out every single other thing.

It's not that you can't do any of the things that you crossed out; it's that now you have given yourself permission to not care about them. Chairs? Yes, you probably need them. But unless they somehow made it onto your green-pen list, you have magically been freed from worrying about chair covers or memorizing the different kinds of chairs you can rent in increasing order of price (folding, banquet, bent wood, Chiavari). Why? Because it does not really matter to you. And when all is said and done, it really won't matter.

Remember What You Care About

In this chapter, I made you write down more than a few things: the list of your crazy, wild dreams, the vibe of the party you want, and your tentative wedding plan. I asked you to find out what your families cared about and to write that down. Plus, I made you work through that long wedding-magazine list, circle the stuff that made you happy, and cross off the stuff you didn't care about. Here is the key step: keep these lists. Pin the lists to your bulletin board, or put them somewhere you can easily find them. We're about to dive into the nitty-gritty parts of wedding planning, and sometimes what you really want has a way of getting lost under what you think you have to have. You're going to need some touchstones of sanity during this process.

THE PRACTICAL BRIDE REMEMBERS . . .

- Take some time to enjoy being engaged before you plunge into the insanity of wedding planning.

- Remember the joy. Your wedding celebrates a truly wonderful, life-changing event. So if it's not making you happy? Chuck it.

- Learn how to say no to what you don't want, and yes to what makes you grin.

- Engagement is a transition. Take some time to talk to your partner about what you want out of your marriage. And remember, if you fight a bit? That's normal.

- Brainstorm with your partner to figure out what you want in your wedding before starting to listen to anyone (and everyone) else's opinion.

- Put this on your fridge, or write it on your forearm: "I will not remember what my wedding looked like; I will remember what it felt like."

- Really internalize that mass media wedding pictures (and yes, that includes blogs) don't represent, well, reality.

- Figure out what your wedding non-negotiables are before you talk to your family, and if you need to, be firm with them that these items are off the table for discussion.

- Ask and really listen to what your families' needs are for your wedding.

- It's not your day—it belongs to everyone who loves you—but it is your wedding. Let this shape your compromises (and do make compromises).

- Before you start planning, make a list of what you really care about and why. Now you've liberated yourself to not care about everything else you are "supposed" to care about.

vows before the justice of the peace. Life has a way of making room for the fundamentally hopeful act of uniting two people into a new family. You just have to know how to dream up the wedding magic. Once you break outside the box of weddings as prescribed by popular culture, anyone in any circumstance, with any amount of money, can make a simple, earth-shatteringly joyful, heartfelt wedding happen.

Popular wedding culture has inscribed a very limited view of weddings in our collective brains. This view has nothing to do with hundreds of years of history (which we'll discuss in Chapter 3). If you pick up a wedding magazine or scroll through a popular wedding blog, you'll see a few types of weddings repeated over and over and over: the church wedding, the hotel wedding, the winery wedding, the estate wedding, the beach-resort wedding, the museum wedding, and more recently, the rustic-chic barn wedding. Though all of these weddings are lovely, they can also be expensive and complicated. But they appear to be your only choices, so many of us spend hours and hours trying to figure out how we can make them work for us, whether we like them or not.

But! It turns out there are options. There are so, so many options: practical options, simple options, affordable options, and—best—subvert-the-paradigm options (because yes, you can totally make that hotel wedding work for you). In this chapter, we'll discuss the fundamental building blocks of a wedding—the who, where, when, and how. First, we'll look at your guest list, then we'll walk through the wedding venue search and discuss the delights of morning and off-season weddings. Finally, we'll discuss the central question of planning a wedding reception: "How are we going to feed these people?" Historically, weddings were a ceremony and then some sort of celebration. And when you simplify it to that level, you have a world of choices.

Megan and Paul's Wedding That Paul Planned

BY MEGAN KONGAIKA

I'll be honest. I began planning my wedding before I was even out of the womb. From the dress, to the walk down the aisle with my dad, to the entire town of guests, to our first dance, to the party favors—it was all orchestrated (in my head) like a MasterCard commercial. But then things changed.

Paul proposed two weeks before Christmas. Two months later, my father lost his yearlong battle with cancer. This devastating event left us all exhausted and grieving. All my life I'd looked forward to planning a wedding, but following my father's death it felt difficult and awkward to even attempt to muster excitement about doing so. I also didn't want to put off the wedding, as Paul had seen me through the most difficult year of my life, and I was ready to officially begin our journey together.

So, with the exception of four contributions, Paul planned our wedding.

My husband and I are very different. He's a Pacific Islander (born and raised in Tonga) and fully embodies the spirit of the island. "Laid-back" doesn't even begin to describe it. In contrast, I'm a Montana girl who would prefer to plan my own surprise birthday party. By that I mean I would lead guests in the birthday song if no one appeared to be making it happen. He prefers to simply let things play out—to "see how it goes." I lean toward a more commandant approach.

Given that information, it came as a surprise to some (hi, Mom!) that I was willing to give up control and hand over the reins to Paul. Sure, I fought back a grand mal seizure when my husband said we didn't need to have a guest list, but it got easier.

Other than buying two plane tickets to Hawaii (contribution #1), inviting our closest friends and family (contribution #2), buying a $150 dress online (contribution #3), and saying a Hail Mary that, at the end of the day, Paul and I would end up married (contribution #4), I pretty much left it up to him.

On the morning of our wedding, I was fairly quiet on the way to the church as I pondered how this whole thing might come

[continues]

together. With the exception of my few contributions, I'd put the entire day in the hands of Paul and his very traditional Tongan family. Secretly I wondered and worried whether I'd be able to hide any disappointment I thought I was bound to feel by not having things go exactly as I'd always imagined. I'd confessed this concern to my mother the day before. She calmly grabbed my shoulders and whispered, "It will be glorious. It will be just as it should be." She trusted him. I decided to follow suit.

When I walked into the church, I fought back tears as I took in the entire scene. There were flowers, and bows, and music piping through the church sound system. Traditional Tongan tapa clothes lined the floor like royal rugs. The reception area was completely set up, and more than forty of my fiancé's relatives were there to greet us warmly with welcoming smiles.

Before I knew it, Paul and I were decked out in traditional Tongan wedding gear. I met our ring bearer (surprise!) seconds before we walked down the aisle. I met our vocalist (surprise!). Then the music started, and it was showtime.

As my stepdad of twenty-five years walked me down the aisle, I thought to myself, "Paul pulled it off. He really did it." My closest friends and family were surrounding me, the man of my dreams, who'd made it all happen, was waiting for me at the end of the aisle, and everything was just as it was supposed to have been. Paul and his family had given me the most wonderful wedding I could have ever imagined. *This* was the moment that mattered.

When people ask me about my wedding day, I tell them that despite being unable to take credit for nearly all of it, there isn't one thing I would have changed.

So, thank you to my husband, Paul, for planning our wedding. It was nothing like I'd pictured it to be all my life. It was better.

Who: The Guest List—How Hard Can It Be?

Let's start at the beginning. Before you do anything else (like pick a venue), you need to have a rough idea of how many people you plan to invite. My suggestion is that you start the conversation by asking, "Whom do we love? Who *must* be there?" And then work backward till you have a number. The trick is to figure out how many people you want around you on your wedding day, and then figure out how you can afford to celebrate with them. There is nothing wrong with getting together the two hundred people you love most in the world and feeding them cake and punch on a Sunday afternoon in the park. Do not listen to anyone who tells you that you must cut your guest list to afford a wedding. The most important thing is to gather the people who love you. Once you do that, the details will iron themselves out.

As you're working, keep in mind that for many couples, the seemingly simple project of figuring out whom to invite, and then inviting them, is one of the most fraught parts of planning. Guest lists are the single biggest outward manifestation of the power struggles that accompany a wedding. (Who gets to invite whom? What sort of a wedding is this anyway? What do you mean I can't invite whomever I want?) In addition, guest lists tend to expose the rift between how you wish things were and reality. You love so-and-so, but you haven't seen her in years. You were absolutely sure so-and-so was going to come, but then he bowed out. Unfortunately, there is no magic solution for this other than crying it out and discussing it. The best I can tell you is that when all is said and done, the people who show up to support you on your wedding day will be the important ones.

Tips for Creating Your
Guest List with Minimal Tears

Building a guest list can be tricky. So before you start developing the list, here are some issues to think through.

- Who is paying? If your parents are helping pay for the wedding, it's reasonable to expect that they will want to invite people they care about (in fact, it's reasonable to expect this even if they are not paying). That said, when accepting the money, it's fair for you to set some limits on what that guest list will look like, because no matter what, you want to get married surrounded by people who know you and love you.

- Knowing you versus knowing *of* you. Your parents have their own social life. They have friends from work who don't know you at all, and they have old friends you haven't seen since you were a toddler. It can be helpful to give your parents general guidelines about whom you feel comfortable having at your wedding, but also, make exceptions. Sometimes your parents do know best, and the most fun wedding guest will be the one you haven't seen since you were three.

- Business versus personal. If you, your partner, or your parents are businesspeople or have very active social calendars, there may be expectations of inviting people who are owed social or business favors. It is perfectly fair to decide that you are limiting invitations to people with close personal ties to you or your family, but it's good to discuss these constraints up front.

- Are you still close? It can be tempting to want to invite everyone who's invited you to his or her wedding, or old friends from high school whom you haven't seen in ages. But that isn't mandatory. When shaping the guest list, think about whom you are close to currently, not just whom you wish you were still in touch with.

- Are you allowing dates? This is a party you are throwing and paying for. You are under no obligation to invite people you don't know (unless we're talking about your friend's long-term partner, and then you are totally obligated). However, you do need to make sure that single friends are taken care of once they arrive—for goodness' sake, sit them next to someone fun.

Troubleshooting

Once you've gotten your guest list down on paper, you still may face a few small problems, most of which have sensible solutions.

- You have more people you want to invite than you can possibly afford. A European system for organizing weddings is to invite a core group of people to the ceremony, invite more people to the meal, and invite everyone you know to the dancing. Though this is hard to pull off without hurt feelings in the States, it's worth borrowing from that tradition if you're having a smaller wedding due to budget constraints. If you're having a wedding at the courthouse, feel free to invite everyone over to your house for celebratory pizza and beer. If you're having a small wedding, throw an after-party in a bar, and show up in your wedding dress. While people probably won't fly in for the wedding after-party, chances are, your friends who live in town will be delighted at the opportunity to celebrate with you.

- You have no idea how many people are actually going to show up. Turnout for a wedding varies based on a whole lot of factors, but the primary variable to consider is what percentage of your guest list is local. Wedding planners will tell you that a good rule of thumb is to expect a 75 percent turnout. That said, 90 percent of our guest list consisted of out-of-towners, and we had more like a 60 percent turnout. So take a good, hard look at your guest list and estimate who will show. Try not to invite more probably-will-shows than your venue can fit, at least in the first round of invitations. Which brings me to the fact that you absolutely can invite people in tiers. We sent out more invitations than save-the-dates once we realized what our turnout looked like. So if it helps, make an A-list, a B-list, and a C-list. No one should ever know what list they were on, but if half of the A-list can't come, well, the B-listers are a pretty fun crowd.

- You have no idea when to send the invitations. Classic etiquette tells you that invitations should go out six weeks before the event, but in the day and age of far-flung friends and family and busy social calendars, I recommend that you send your invitations a little in advance of that (unless you're planning a wedding with a short engagement period, in which case, go you!). You can send save-the-dates up to a year in advance, or you can skip them altogether and just call people. They'll still save the date, and they'll get to squeal with delight and chat with you. Everyone wins!

- Wedding guests keep inviting extra guests. There are two common guest list problems that, luckily enough, have exactly the same solution. The first is wedding guests inviting their own wedding guests, and the second is people trying to bring children to your child-free wedding. Blessedly, etiquette has provided us with a simple solution to both of these vexing problems: the envelope. The rules are the same: the people invited are the people whose names are written on the envelope. So if you're not inviting children, you don't put the children's name on the envelope. If you're not inviting your sister's erstwhile fling, well, the same rule applies. Unfortunately, this sometimes needs to be followed up with a firm but polite phone call to say rather sweetly, "While we're delighted that you'd like to bring your child/usually drunk teenage boyfriend, I'm afraid we can only accommodate you at our late-night black-tie cocktail party." That said, if you're not inviting kids (or dates), keep it uniform; you can't invite only kids (or dates) you like. And if you're not inviting kids, try not to have an afternoon wedding at the zoo with clowns making balloon animals and barrels of punch. Kids would be sad to miss that, and that would be understandable.

The People You Need Are the Ones Who Show Up

In the depth of wedding planning, having faith that you are making the right choices with your guest list can be hard. We had some painful moments: close friends who canceled on the wedding with little reason, loved ones who couldn't come due to financial constraints, confusion over whom we should invite. In the end, I wish I'd known how it would feel. When you walk down the aisle, the people who are there are the ones who matter—those people, and the people you hold in your heart.

Where: The Quest for a Wedding Venue

Now that you have an idea of what kind of wedding you and your partner want, your families' thoughts on the subject, and at least a vague guess as to how many people you plan on inviting, it's time to look for a wedding venue. Please heed me when I say you should look for a wedding venue *before you do anything else.* I'm not generally one for hard and fast rules, but in this case, it's practical. Looking for a wedding venue can be a real pain, and it's tempting to want to skip that step for a while and move on to the fun things, like dress shopping. The thing is, where and when you hold your wedding (the location, the time of day, the season) will dictate most of the rest of your planning. You don't want to run off and buy a dress you love, only to find that your indie-eloping-in-Vegas sheath doesn't work at all at the garden-in-the-middle-of-a-forest wedding you end up throwing.

Though picking a venue can feel immense, it's not a life-or-death decision. Catherine Sly, who married in a simple civil service before holding her reception in a hotel function room in Brighton, England, told me, "We only looked at one reception venue. People asked me if I didn't feel like I should look around more, but I just thought, 'We're having a party there, not buying the place.'" So stop stressing out, and get cracking. Once you've picked the venue, it will feel as if a huge weight has lifted off your shoulders and like this wedding thing is for real.

The Traditional Wedding Venue

A logical place to start the search is often in traditional wedding venue directories, both online and in print. This will tend to limit your search to the classic wedding location, for better or worse. Venues that cater to weddings tend to be relatively pricey, require long lead times, and often have complicated contracts. They do, however, have their strengths. If you want a dance floor, staff who know exactly what they are doing, or an all-inclusive wedding package, a traditional wedding venue is probably the way to go. And sometimes letting someone else do the dirty work for you is worth the extra cost. Lisa Dennis said, "To keep my sanity, it was worth it to us to pay the price to have our reception at a place that would cover all the food, the setup, and the cleanup. Worrying about that could've killed me." Know your limitations. If you want a full-service venue, then by all means, your sanity is worth it.

However, it's important to walk into a traditional wedding venue prepared to ask the right questions. Trust me, nothing is quite so fun as finding out you just paid $4,000 for a totally empty room with no staff.

THINGS TO THINK ABOUT WHEN
LOOKING AT TRADITIONAL WEDDING VENUES

- Are tables and chairs provided? Do not assume they are, and do not assume that renting them will be cheap. Find out exactly what is provided and who sets up and tears down.

- What is the staff situation? What staff members are included in your flat fee, and what will they take care of? Are there additional staff members they suggest (or require) you to hire? Should you expect to tip staff?

- Can you bring your own alcohol? Few things will save you more money than being able to provide your own wine and beer. Instead of paying $12 a cocktail (ouch!), you can pay $12 for a whole bottle of wine. Wedding venues know this, and it's a rare venue that will let you do it. So! Do your research. Paying a little more for a venue that will let you bring the booze will often save you tons of money in the final calculation.

- Are you locked into a catering contract? Many venues either require that you use an on-site caterer or provide you with a list of preferred caterers. This isn't always a terrible thing, but it can be more expensive and somewhat limiting, so it's good to know about it up front. In particular, keep a keen eye out for venues that allow you to use only one caterer. When there is no competition for the business, it can be harder for you to keep costs down.

- Hidden fees, hidden fees, hidden fees. Is there a cake-cutting fee? A corkage fee? A cleanup fee? An "oh my God, you're charging me for *what*" fee? Hidden fees are standard industry practice. Ask questions about additional fees before you sign a contract (and for more on contracts, please do yourself a favor and see Chapter 5).

Other Places to Throw a Fabulous Party (That Happens to Celebrate Your Marriage)

Maybe you want to get a little adventurous. Maybe you want to save money, or maybe you just want to color outside the wedding lines. You've decided that a traditional wedding venue is not for you and want to explore other options.

Weddings, as presented by the wedding industry, are parties with a very strict formula: ceremony, cocktails and appetizers, sit-down dinner, cake cutting, first dance, dance party, send-off. We'll discuss in Chapter 3 the fact that none of this is particularly traditional, but when everyone tells you it's the Way Things Are Done, it's easy to start feeling trapped. We start thinking that we need a ceremony site, a place to have cocktails, and a dance floor. But the truth is, weddings don't need any of these prescribed elements.

So stop thinking about throwing a wedding, and start thinking about throwing a party. What kind of parties do you normally throw or attend? Do your tastes run to dinner parties? Picnics? Gatherings in religious social halls? Bashes in the middle of the desert? All-night dance parties? Excellent. Now start considering the size of your wedding and how you would throw those parties if you needed to make them a little bigger. Where would you throw a non-wedding party? What would the location be? Now you're talking. So let's discuss specifics, which will take some sleuthing and, yes, some compromises.

Parks: Trade Your Wedding Planner for a Park Ranger

We got married in a wedding venue located on an enormous piece of local parkland, and we could not have made a better choice. The key advantages were price, stunning scenery, not having to deal with wedding people (just park rangers), and the fact that every penny we paid went to supporting our local parks. Of course, parks have their drawbacks. As government-owned entities, there are often very strict regulations and time limits you have to adhere to. For us that felt like a compromise, but we realized that we didn't think about the regulations for a hot second on our wedding day (and the four-year-olds still ended up sneaking off to play in the flower beds, allowed or not).

You'd be surprised at the number of traditional wedding venues located in parks. But beyond that, look into picnic venues you can rent for the day. You can fancy-up a picnic site with white tablecloths and candles, bring in food from a local restaurant, and have an elegant outdoor dinner-party wedding. You can throw up a piñata and some Mexican paper flags, rent a taco truck, and have a fiesta wedding. The bottom line is, with a picnic space, you have an affordable blank canvas to do almost anything.

And finally, consider saying your vows in a park and having the celebration elsewhere. Many national and state parks have beautiful overlook points, gazebos, or spots by a lake, where you can have your friends and loved ones gather while you say your vows, and then dash off to a local restaurant or backyard to celebrate.

Restaurants: Just Look Around Your Neighborhood

Though it's perfectly possible to have a really expensive wedding in a really fancy restaurant, there are also tons of smaller neighborhood restaurants that are delighted to host weddings, affordably. Start looking at restaurants you like to go to regularly, along with cafés and, yes, even bars. Look at that Mexican place with the big back room; look at the brunch place where you like to go on Sunday mornings; look at that pub with the exposed brick walls. Heck, look at the big chain restaurant with the back room that does balloon bouquets for birthday parties—who's to say you couldn't make some seriously unexpected wedding magic happen there (with lots of giant balloons)? The best part is finding out how thrilled many of these businesses will be to get to host a wedding. Instead of being gouged with endless hidden fees, you'll suddenly be dealing with people who are overjoyed and flattered that you would think of hosting one of the most joyful events of your life in their establishment.

Cara Winter, who held her reception in a farm-to-table restaurant in Brooklyn, explained the advantages of a restaurant wedding this way: "If you're considering a completely DIY decorated party in the parish hall, consider this: if just explaining the aesthetic to your mom leads to a stress-induced meltdown and you've never actually made anything by hand before, you might want to evaluate whether the extra couple thousand to do it at a chic no-decorations-needed restaurant is worth it. My sanity was worth about $1,850." Restaurants are brilliant, not just because the food is bound to be good, but because they come pre-decorated. You just show up and have a party.

Social Halls: Spinning Straw into Gold

We have all gotten so indoctrinated with the idea that weddings happen in beautiful wedding *venues*, that it seems a bit of a throwback to consider having your reception (and even your ceremony) in a social hall. But. It is always worthwhile to look around you to see what social halls you have at your disposal, and then figure out if you can use a little joy and style to make the place glorious. Morgan Turigan, who married in Calgary, Canada, did just that: "We had a cheapish wedding. It was not full of charming details or at a beautiful venue or full of indie spirit. It was at a plain hall with minimal decoration, and it was so full of love and family that I couldn't stop beaming." In the end, it's not the beauty of the wedding venue that makes the party; it's your joy, and the joy of the people who have gathered around you. If the way you can afford to get everyone you love in one place is by hosting your reception at a public social hall, do it. Yes, some of these places are less than beautiful, but you'd be surprised what some flowers and joy can do to a place.

And Anywhere Else You Can Imagine

You can throw a wedding just about anywhere if you're willing to think outside the box. I've heard of weddings held at summer camps, youth hostels, rented vacation homes, apple orchards, and public beaches. The list is only limited by your imagination and your moxie, so get dreaming.

The Simplest Weddings

When we look at the history of weddings (which we will do in more depth in Chapter 3), we see a long tradition of simple weddings. For hundreds of years, weddings in the United States took place in people's homes. During World War II, a huge number of weddings took place at the courthouse with the bride in her best clothes, always with flowers. We've lost track of these simple traditions in a flurry of ever bigger and more complicated weddings. But there is something profoundly beautiful about these simple weddings. They can be done quickly and easily, allowing the focus to be on the love between two people.

At-Home and Backyard Weddings

Weddings are (or should be) a slightly more dignified version of the parties you already throw, so if you or your parents have a home you feel comfortable entertaining in, you have a home that is perfect for a small wedding. Emma Straub, who had a simple wedding in Manhattan, told me, "We ended up with about thirty people in my parents' dining room. I wore my mother's dress and a piece of tulle the size of a pumpkin on my head. It was packed and warm and perfect—I was surrounded by people I love. What could be better?" And that's the magic of the at-home wedding. It's not fussy, but having the people you love in a place you call home is its own kind of wonderful.

It's easy to do a little research about at-home weddings and get scared. I've read articles that say at-home weddings nearly always end with renovating the home to make it appropriate for guests. This is blatant silliness, unless you call a contractor every time you invite people over for dinner. When preparing your home for your wedding, I'd suggest that you hire a housekeeper to make the place spotless possibly before, and definitely after, the wedding, but that's it. Kathleen Shannon, who got married in her 1920s bungalow in Oklahoma City, said, "Trust me, there was nothing romantic about mopping down our wood floors, sticky with spilled liquor, the morning after our wedding." But beyond making sure your house is clean and you have something to wear, there is not a whole lot that you *must* do, which is incredibly liberating.

You'll need a place to say your vows and a place for your guests to sit (which may well mean procuring extra chairs, either by renting them or borrowing them). You'll need a table to spread food and some space for mingling, or a setup for a small dinner party or luncheon. Homes and backyards offer you a chance to create your wedding from scratch—to decorate as little or as much as you want; to make your own food or have it catered from a local restaurant; to have a dance party on the back patio; to have a formal dinner party in the living room. And in the end, what you'll be left with are the best memories in the world, every time you walk through the door.

The Courthouse Wedding

Courthouse weddings are enjoying something of a resurgence. It's easy to get caught up in thinking you need to make your wedding day complicated and stressful for it to feel special. But your wedding day will be important no matter what, because it's the day you vow to spend your life with another person. Lindsay Whitfield, who had a simple wedding at the courthouse while eight months pregnant, said, "I was worried that without an audience made up of family and friends I wouldn't recognize the solemnity of the moment. But the second I walked down the aisle, saw my husband, and realized what we were about to do, the solemnity and sacredness of the moment overwhelmed me." Courthouse weddings narrow the focus to a ritual that moves couples to the other side—a ritual that makes them a family.

The Elopement

Elopements may be the one remaining taboo of wedding planning. Somehow, the argument goes, weddings are something we do for other people, something we do for the social fabric, and it's selfish to get married privately. You will, of course, not mind if I calmly disagree.

Elopements are not for everyone. If the idea of eloping sounds romantic, but the idea of getting married without those you love around you makes you feel slightly ill, then listen to your gut. But if you realize that planning a wedding is not going to work in your situation, or if your wedding plans have gotten so out of control that you don't recognize them anymore, well, elopements can be wonderful things.

The most brilliant part of eloping is that you don't have to plan it. If you decide to elope, you can toss this book aside (and come back to read Chapter 10 when all is said and done), throw your spreadsheets out the window, and go. Emily Threlkeld, who eloped to New Orleans, said that she initially tried to plan her elopement until she realized that the planned elopement was a contradiction in terms. She said, "I let things go. I turned to Google, and within the week I had ordered a dress, our wedding bands, a pair of shoes. I'd found a minister, a photographer, and a florist. I tried to find a hairdresser in New Orleans and had visions of a fabulous up-do shellacked to my head with a lot of hairspray, but I ended up going with Spin Pins instead." Not only is there no planning to worry about, but there are no rules to follow either. Though elopements traditionally are just the bride and the groom, they don't have to be. Jessica Flaherty married in a beach town in Maine, right before Christmas with both mothers in attendance. She told me, "We mulled the idea of elopement over for a few days and decided

that despite how romantic a true dictionary definition of eloping sounded, we are both children of single moms, and our
mothers meant too much to us and sacrificed too much for us
both to be excluded." You're eloping because it's right for you.
So for goodness' sake, if you want to bring some people you love
with you, do it.

With elopements, even more than with regular weddings,
you have to come face-to-face with the fact that your decisions
might upset people in your lives. And that's hard. Part of getting
married is forming a new family unit and prioritizing the needs
of that new family. Lindsay Whitfield wrote her parents a letter
explaining their choice to elope, and said, "I hoped that they
would understand that we were doing things in a way that was
right for us." In a sense, this is true whether you elope or not.
But knowing that does not make it easy to deal with hurt feelings. Jessica Flaherty said, "I am relatively unfazed, and I am
still married despite the limited discontent. I appreciate that
people may be disappointed to not share our day with us, but I
hope they all know they were there in spirit." Even with some
family displeasure, for women who went with their heart, the
rewards of eloping were worth the limited pain. Lindsay Whitfield told me that even a year later, when having trouble sleeping at night she would "replay our wedding day in my head and
smile myself to sleep."

Elopement is not for the faint of heart. It takes firmness of
purpose to fly in the face of Everything That Is Expected and
run off to get married with no fuss and no bother. But if you
know in your heart of hearts that elopement is for you? Be
brave. And remember that you can throw a huge party later to
celebrate your marriage, and you can throw an anniversary
party any year that you want to celebrate what really matters—
the family you made together.

When: Can You Get Legally Married in the Morning?

The companion question to "*Where* will we have this wedding?" is of course "*When* will we have this wedding?" These days, most of us are convinced that the way to get married is to have a summer evening wedding followed by an all-night dance party. I, for one, wanted to dance until three a.m. in my wedding shoes, on a glorious summer night. But life caught up with me. The reality is that the most popular times to have weddings (summer, evening, and Saturdays) are also the most expensive times to have weddings. And although you hear less about them, off-season weddings, morning weddings, and weeknight weddings all have their advantages—and I don't just mean the advantage of relative affordability.

Morning and Afternoon Weddings

As someone who had a morning wedding against her will and ended up loving it, let me give you the full scoop about the non-evening wedding. There are obvious drawbacks to the morning wedding: you'll have to get up early; your prewedding preparation will be a little rushed; you won't dance the night away (at least not at your reception). But there are a multitude of advantages. It's often possible to save quite a bit of money on morning weddings: you can get venues that would otherwise be booked up; you can negotiate discounts with vendors; you can serve more affordable food; people drink less alcohol. But the advantages don't stop there. The light is beautiful, and if you're getting married in a scenic spot, daylight allows you to enjoy the view. Also, it's a well-kept secret that older generations like early-in-the-day weddings. They don't need to worry about staying up late, and they will have the energy to chat with all of their friends. As for the younger generation, well, if you're drinking and dancing, your friends are going to join you. But none of that compares to the magic of after the wedding. When your wedding ends at three or four in the afternoon, you have the rest of the day to bliss out with your new spouse, or go bar hopping in your wedding dress (the only time in your life you'll ever have an excuse to do that).

Getting Married on a Weekday

Another tried-and-true way of making a wedding more affordable is the weekday wedding. The easiest way to get married on a weekday is to plan a Friday afternoon or evening wedding, but weddings can happen any day of the week. Weekday weddings are, however, a bit like destination weddings: when you ask people to take time off work to attend your ceremony, let them off the hook straightaway. If they can come, you'll be delighted; if they can't, you'll fully understand. That said, if you're planning a small wedding, celebrating on a weekday is a fabulous way to feel like the whole world belongs to you. With everyone at work, it's just you and your loved ones, celebrating your huge new commitment.

Off-Season Weddings

Looking at wedding media, it's easy to get sucked into the idea that all beautiful weddings happen at the height of summer with the sun blazing down and abundant flowers everywhere. But an off-season wedding can save you a sizable amount of money (on both the wedding and honeymoon) and be beautiful. Summer brides don't get things like tights, or fir branches, or piles of autumn leaves, or snow. And they don't get to celebrate their anniversary as a beacon of light in a dark part of the year. Yes, they get warm weather, but that's hardly everything.

How: Food—No, It Doesn't Need to Be Dinner

Once you've gotten a rough count for your guest list, sorted out your venue, and picked the date for your wedding, the next hurdle is food. Food is expensive, and the kind of food you serve tends to set the tone for the kind of party you're going to have (a cake-and-punch reception is super fun, but totally different from a sit-down, three-course meal).

When I told my mom that I wanted to have a meal and dancing at my wedding, she looked at me like I'd lost my mind. Thirty years ago, the only people she knew who had dinner and dancing at their reception were fantastically wealthy. But by the time I got married, most of the weddings I went to had sit-down meals, and I figured that was the way to have a ragingly fun party. I was wrong. (And in the end we compromised on a buffet lunch.)

No matter how popular the dinner-and-dancing reception is, you have tons of options. You can serve a meal, but make it breakfast, brunch, or lunch (which are often less expensive). You can serve appetizers only, or just cake and punch (which is arguably one of the *most* traditional receptions). But beyond that, you have lots of ways to source your food. You can make traditional catering work for you, or find alternative catering sources (like restaurants). For the more ambitious among us, in Chapter 6 we'll discuss self-catering. No matter what tool you use, you absolutely can find a way to serve delicious food on a budget that is right for you. Stop worrying that if you color outside the prescribed wedding food lines people won't have fun. "If you're catering your own wedding, and you're worried it's gonna be a bust . . . don't," said Liz Moorhead. The people who love you will love you no matter what you serve them, and they will show up ready to party. Your job is to figure out a way to keep yourself sane and solvent, while serving food that makes you happy.

How to Hack Traditional Catering

There are many wonderful things to be said about traditional caterers: they know what they are doing; you pay them so you never have to think about your wedding food again; they do all the setup and teardown themselves; and their food is good (right? Because if it's bad, you'd better not be paying them cash money). That said, traditional catering can also be insanely expensive and sometimes feels predictable (we have to serve chicken with a vegetable and bread? Just like every other wedding ever? Sad trombone). So if you use traditional catering, it's important to remember that you can hack the system to make it work for you.

- Ask about less traditional food choices. Caterers are quick to recommend the meat entrée with two sides and bread because that's what most people want, but you should feel free to get creative. We had our caterer prepare a non-meat-centric Middle Eastern spread. The food was delicious and unexpected, and we were able to shave a little off the cost by not preparing pricey cuts of meat.

- Differentiate between expensive food and tasty food. Some caterers specialize in food that looks fancy: filet mignon, anything served by waiters in black tie, wedding cakes as art with a side of ice sculpture. Expect these caterers to mark up their prices. There are also caterers who specialize in food that looks less fancy but is in fact super tasty. Don't be suckered into thinking that elaborate food is the best food. If you look beyond the ice sculptures, you often can find better-tasting solutions that are more affordable.

- See if you can provide some of your own extras. Your caterer may be willing to provide a fancy wedding cake—for a fee. This may not be something they make in-house, but something they contract out to a cake maker. If so, they will charge you for the hassle. So start chatting about what extras you can provide on your own. Our caterers let us provide our own cake (and were delighted to not have to bother with it themselves), as well as our own alcohol. This saved us some serious money.

Yes, Of Course Restaurants Cater

The hidden-in-plain-view secret about wedding catering is that (wait for it . . .) you don't need to use a wedding caterer. If you have a venue that is flexible on catering options, you can look into getting your food from a variety of sources, including but not limited to:

- Restaurants

- Gourmet grocery stores (party platters)

- Food carts (taco trucks, etc.)

- Pizzerias (yes, I said it)

You can get food from any restaurant or food-service establishment willing to take a large order in advance. If you use this option, you usually still need to set up and tear down the food service on your own, as well as take care of renting tables, chairs, and plates. But self-catering is a lot easier when you're not doing the actual catering. Also, ordering food from a restaurant can cost a fraction of a full-service catering contract.

Dream It . . . Do It

When putting together the building blocks for your wedding, it's easy to get stuck. You think you have to have a hundred people, or a dance floor, or an evening wedding, or to serve dinner. Even when you realize that you just can't make your wedding fit into the prescribed vision, you keep trying to make it work, because you think you don't have a choice. A wedding just *is* a big, formal, seated dinner thing, no avoiding that fact.

But that's not true. A wedding is a party, and it's as simple as that. Sometimes you just need permission to dream and color outside the celebration lines. Allow your wedding to be what it needs to be. Maybe it's a dance party in the middle of the desert; maybe it's a last-minute elopement; maybe it's planned by your husband, and nothing like what you expected. So step back, loosen the reins, and let your wedding happen. I suspect you'll dream up something excellent.

- Once you break outside the box of weddings as prescribed by popular culture, anyone, in any circumstance, with any amount of money, can make a wedding happen.

- Formulating your guest list can be a complex dance of balancing the needs of many people, not to mention dealing with logistics. But when all is said and done, remember that the people you need are the ones who show up.

- Even though the venue search can feel overwhelming, it's important to pick your venue before you jump into planning the rest of your wedding. The time and place set the tone for everything else.

- When looking at traditional venues, watch for hidden fees, and ask lots of questions.

- Many big cities have affordable public wedding venues in parks, or you can rent a picnic spot or overlook point.

- Neighborhood restaurants, bars, cafés, and even chain restaurants with event spaces can offer tasty food and affordable style.

- Social halls may sound old-school, but there is almost nothing a few glasses of champagne and delirious joy (not to mention a bevy of helpful friends) can't fix.

- If you're thinking of a small wedding, consider embracing the at-home or courthouse wedding, or even eloping.

- Consider having your wedding at a less popular time—during the day, midweek, or in the fall or winter. Chances are, your wedding will cost less and be quirky and beautiful.

- You don't need to serve a full meal during your reception, but if you do, remember to look at less traditional options for food service.

- Stop trying to force your wedding into the box of How Everyone Else Does It, and just let it be what it is. It's going to be excellent.

Hannah & Frederick, 1974
BY FRED AND HANNAH KEENE

Hannah and I got married at the high altar in Grace Cathedral in San Francisco with five Episcopal priests celebrating the Eucharist early in the winter on the Feast of the Holy Innocents.

Elaborate, yes. Expensive, not really. The five priests were close personal friends, most about our age. We asked them to wear their fanciest, most colorful vestments. A friend printed copies of the liturgy so everybody knew what to say. I asked my brother to be head usher; the other ushers and our attendants were close friends. We chose the hymns and even included a Christmas carol. Other friends baked the bread for Communion. We chose a Zinfandel for the wine and asked the priests to give big sips to the recipients. The wedding ceremony itself takes no more than twenty minutes, so we chose to have Communion. It is optional but emphasizes the idea that a wedding incorporates a married couple into the community. We are big on that kind of thing.

The Christmas decorations were still up in the cathedral; the only flowers we needed were corsages for our mothers and bouquets for Hannah and her attendants. We did not belong to the cathedral congregation, so the use of the building cost a couple hundred dollars, but a verger (a custodian, wearing vestments) came with it. We decided to hire one of the cathedral organists for another hundred or two. This did not seem like very much, and he could play anything we wanted, including, for the recessional, some heavy-duty Bach that matched one of the hymn tunes. We had the receiving line at the back of the church so we could greet our friends, and they could start partying as soon as they got to the reception. The organist rang change for half an hour. The photographer had shot my sister's wedding two years earlier (the reception had been in my parents' backyard) and charged us the same price even though he was from out of town and had to travel. (His wife wanted an excuse for a trip to San Francisco.)

Hannah did all the heavy lifting in putting the wedding together. In the late spring she had agreed to marry me, so she had about six months. I had just finished my degree, and my first full-time job was on the East Coast. It started in late August, so I was not around to help her. Both of her parents worked full-time, so although they paid for the wedding and set some limits, the wedding belonged to Hannah. However, I was around when she got

[continues]

her wedding dress in the early summer. It was a winter dress with long sleeves, and was marked down 50 percent to $150 at one of the high-end department stores, which fit right into the budget. The dress was actually a little short and could not be lengthened, so Hannah wore perfectly flat ballet-style satin bedroom slippers to disguise the shortness.

Hannah's parents arranged for the reception; the ceremony was ours. The reception cost more than $1,000, a lot of money in those days, but it covered the venue, the food, and the setup and service. We served hors d'oeuvres, wedding cake, and champagne punch. Hannah's mother had given us the choice of limiting the guest list or eliminating the champagne service. We gave up the champagne. We bought the cake at a local coffeehouse, now defunct, where one of the bakers had trained at the fanciest bakery in San Francisco. It cost $100, a good price for a good cake. Different layers were different flavors, an innovation back then. They baked a sample cake for free; Hannah had them write "Happy Birthday, Mom," and used it for her mother's birthday.

The reception was held at the Marines Memorial Club. My father had been a career officer in the Marine Corps and a charter member of the club; Meg used his dress saber to cut her cake, just as Hannah had used her grandfather's military sword to cut hers. Hannah's parents also were members of the club; her father had been an army officer.

My sister's church wedding and backyard reception two years prior had cost $1,000. Ours cost $2,000, and we did not feel that it was outrageous. That $2,000 would be about $8,700 now, due to inflation. On the other hand, the price of duplicating our wedding would now cost more than $40,000.

The 1970s was an era when "alternative" could mean many things. We took the standard service and pushed the envelope as far as we could; our parents were distinctly dubious about its showiness. And that did not even include the Episcopal chaplain to UC Berkeley carrying the Bible into the midst of the congregation so the Gospel could be read by the pastor of the Berkeley Free Church, one of the most radical priests of the '60s. Alternative is as alternative does. For $2,000 we were able to get the wedding we wanted. We like to dress up, put on a big show, and have a party. And even the local vendors and the staffs of the cathedral and the Marines Memorial Club seemed to have a good time. And the best part? We've had over thirty-six years of a great marriage as well.

Interestingly, most of the significant changes in the American way of tying the knot have been made opaque. There is a multibillion-dollar industry devoted to telling us that things have always been exactly the way they are this second, and we need to buy everything on offer because "this is the way it's always been done," and "changing things would be thumbing our nose at tradition and all the generations that have gone before us." The thing is, this is not strictly true.

I think it's empowering to know a little bit about wedding history. That way, when you hear the word "tradition," you'll have a sense of whether what's being referred to is in fact traditional (say, the vows), or is in fact brand-new (say, the unity candle). This will make you much better equipped to take all advice with a grain of salt (or to say, "Actually, Mom, we don't *need* an aisle runner").

Also, it turns out that actual wedding etiquette is remarkably uninterested in your spending boatloads of money. (Who knew?) The goal of this chapter is to help you reclaim *actual* tradition, in a way that's helpful to you.

A Brief History of Weddings in America

Let's start in the early 1800s in the United States. Most weddings during this period took place at home (meaning your at-home or backyard wedding is perhaps the most traditional wedding you could possibly throw). There were a variety of different reasons that weddings took place in the front parlor. For middle-class Protestants, the feeling was that the ritual of marriage should not be fussy and glorified, but simple and held in a place with emotional significance to the parties involved. And for much of the population, there was limited access to churches to get married *in*. So, the parlor wedding was the standard, and these celebrations were generally quiet, small, and informal. These weddings were planned with very little lead time, and generally very little expense. A few weeks' notice was given, the bride wore her best (and not usually white) dress, the family gathered, vows were said, and cake was eaten.

By the mid-nineteenth century, life in America had started to become slightly more ritualized. Wedding ceremonies began moving to churches, making them both more formal and more expensive. Wedding receptions, by and large, were still held at home. It's important to note that at this point in our cultural history, weddings were not parties thrown by professionals. The women in the family were still doing it all: the cooking, the decorating, and often even the sewing of the wedding dress. In fact, most women would have been horrified at the idea of hiring help to do something that was seen as a labor of love. These days we talk about DIY weddings (see Chapter 6) as if they were a newfangled wedding trend, but the fact of the matter is that weddings historically were do-it-together events. Weddings were viewed as deeply personal celebrations, not to be mucked about by professionals (and besides, there was great pride in throwing your daughter a party to celebrate this huge transition in her life).

Professional wedding services began to make an appearance at the turn of the twentieth century, but in ways we wouldn't even recognize now. Making your cake and then sending it to a baker to be professionally decorated? Now we would think of that as DIY and crafty. But at the turn of the twentieth century, this was a huge step in the direction of professionalism. As invitations began to be purchased (newfangled!) and lavish public weddings held by the wealthy became increasingly common, the role of commercialization in weddings became something of a flash point. Was simple better? Were people losing the connection with tradition in favor of showy weddings that parted families from their hard-earned money? It seems that when it comes to grand old wedding traditions, the fight to bring back simple weddings is as traditional as anything else (and more traditional than the aisle runner).

But oddly, it is during the rebellious, hard-drinking, short skirt and lipstick-wearing 1920s that the wedding industry as we know it became visible. During this period of massive social change, an industry was born that marketed weddings as traditional, unchanging, and profoundly conservative. If your daughter is going to get married in a shockingly short, knee-length skirt, and smoke and drink at her reception, it's reassuring to be told how to make her wedding proper. The wedding industry that developed in the 1920s had very little to do with the actual history of small, at-home weddings thrown with little or no professional help. But during an era of change, the idea of "traditional" weddings had an undeniable appeal.

In fact, what emerged in the 1920s was a wedding that bears a lot of resemblance to the weddings we see today. For the first time, most weddings took place in churches, and the receptions moved out of the home and into public social halls. Dancing began to be part of the festivities, along with photography, and the white wedding dress became readily available (off the rack!) to a wide swath of American women. It's a classic chicken-and-egg question: Did the modern wedding industry give birth to the more complicated, more expensive wedding, or was it the other way around? Regardless, with a generation of women marrying in white, something their mothers did not do, brides and mothers needed advice. And as would become a constant, the wedding industry was there to provide advice. Expensive advice. Advice about mostly invented tradition. Expensive tradition.

As the roaring 1920s became the depressed 1930s, you would think the newly formed wedding industry would go into hibernation. But as one of the slogans of the time read, "Love knows no depression!" Thanks to some rather serious marketing efforts, in the 1930s the white wedding became the standard template for weddings and was increasingly available to everyone. In a time of very little money and very little waste, women were buying white wedding dresses that could be reworn, but (with a brief interlude of wartime civil ceremonies excepted) that didn't last long.

And then the war years dawned. With so many men heading off to fight in World War II, marriage rates skyrocketed. Eighty percent of the grooms were in the armed services, so civil ceremonies became a necessity. When your groom is shipping off to war in a week, you hurry down to the courthouse in your best suit or dress (with flowers), celebrate with some punch and cake, and then dash off to spend some time alone. But the wedding industry wasn't going to let everyone off quite that easily (after all, an industry that survived the Depression could make it through a war). Suddenly the rhetoric surrounding weddings changed. The white wedding became deeply patriotic—part of the American way of life everyone was fighting for.

As the war ended and we moved toward the deeply conservative 1950s, it is hardly surprising that weddings got bigger, more formal, and more expensive. In her excellent wedding history book, *All Dressed in White*, Carol McD. Wallace sums up the era this way: "The wedding ceased to be a homemade celebration and became something you bought." She explains, "In the mid-twentieth century . . . what was once optional becomes obligatory." The language of the modern wedding industry emerged, and the wedding became "your big day," and "once in a lifetime." And if it's once in a lifetime, it of course needs to be done *properly*. As the '50s and '60s rolled on, "properly" quickly came to mean a big white dress, an elaborate church wedding, and a lavish catered reception. Though, interestingly enough, the lavish catered reception in the mid-century consisted of tea sandwiches and cake, something today's wedding industry would tell us Cannot Be Done.

During the mid-twentieth century, bigger became bigger became bigger, and then the counterculture 1970s arrived. Marriage became a highly individual choice, not a necessity. People began wanting weddings to illustrate the deepest longings of their soul. Couples began to eschew every form of perceived tradition and got married barefoot and pregnant in a meadow. But strangely enough, while everyone was distracted with counterculture celebrations, mainstream weddings suddenly became more complicated.

You see, if weddings are about the deepest desires of our souls, then wedding industry logic says that they should be personalized. It was in the 1970s that wedding favors were introduced, along with the unity candle. Within ten years, the recommended time for wedding planning expanded from six months to, in 1973, a full year. Which was perfect, because around the same time that getting married in a field became old hat, the 1980s hit. After Diana and Charles's spectacle of a big-sleeved, fairy-tale royal wedding, weddings got enormous. Conspicuous. Expensive. And we started to inch closer to what weddings would become: a mind-bogglingly expensive, not even vaguely traditional production.

Modern Weddings

That brings us to the most complicated and commercial production of all: the modern wedding. Over the past hundred years, one thing has stayed consistent: the accumulation of tradition. We have continued to invent and add rituals, but almost never to subtract them. We started with the cake, vows, and decorations, and slowly added things like the white dress, the double ring ceremony, bridal bouquets, wedding parties, catered receptions, dancing, and photography. And in the past twenty years things have gotten ever more complex and expensive. In the 1970s, weddings started moving toward personalization. These days everything is personalized and everything *means* something. You can't just serve tea sandwiches; you have to think about what serving tea sandwiches says about you. And then you have to research online all the possible kinds of tea sandwiches you could serve and think about how to style them. Nothing is simple, and the Internet is there to provide endless information, which *might* be slowly driving us insane.

And of course, you can't serve tea sandwiches in the first place. As Carol Wallace notes in *All Dressed in White*, "The basic elements of the wedding have been ramped up in the last twenty years. A seated dinner at the reception is now the norm, rather than passed hors d'oeuvres or a buffet. Since no bride and groom today feel the need to rush off to consummate their relationship, wedding receptions tend to last longer, often involving dancing, and there may be a brunch the next day as well, attended by the bride and the groom. In today's mobile society, families and guests often travel long distances for a wedding, so there is distinct pressure to make the event worth their while." In short, weddings have become enormous. We are trying to function under the weight of a hundred years of invented traditions, piled one on top of the other. Each new tradition is invented by an ever bigger, ever stronger wedding industry, ready to tell us that we will regret it if we give up any aspect of the ever larger wedding.

What Is Tradition Anyway?

All this is to say, tradition is a very slippery thing. It's possible to argue that home weddings are traditional, or boozy flapper weddings are traditional, or weddings in social halls with punch and cake are traditional. It's a lot harder to argue that unity

The Registry: It's Not Actually for You

If you're like me, wrapping your mind around the registry might be hard. Part of your brain screams, "We're engaged! Free stuff! Hooray!" and part of your brain wonders why finding a life partner entitles you to plates, especially when you already have plates. Here is what it took me a long time to figure out: the registry is not for you. In fact, the registry has nothing to do with your wedding. Your registry is for your guests and for your marriage.

When guests go to a wedding, they want a way to participate. They don't just want to participate in the party (because to do that, they can just get drunk and do the conga line). They want to find a way to show their support for your marriage. Your wedding day is your first day together as a formal family in the eyes of society, and all the people gathered around with fierce hopes and dreams for you understand that. They know that getting married is easy, but building a life together is hard. They want to support you in the hard part.

The registry is like a barn raising. It gives your guests a time-honored way to tell you that they are with you for the long haul. When you get gifts of sturdy stoneware plates to replace the chipped thrift-store dishes in your cupboards, your loved ones are not being materialistic. They're tangibly showing their love to you through plates that will make it through fights, and moves, and (possibly) kids. They want to show their love for you with plates that you'll take with you to the retirement home.

So no matter what decisions you make about your registry, remember this: you're not getting gifts and cash because you somehow deserve it. You're getting gifts and cash because people are showing their love. The registry isn't about the wedding, and it isn't about you. It's about letting your friends and loved ones build a home for you. It's about letting them love you.

candles and wedding favors are traditional, but that doesn't stop people from trying. If something is done often enough, the wedding industry can convince us that it's actual tradition, with an actual historical connection, and that we'd be insulting our mothers and our grandmothers if we didn't do it (even if they'd never heard of it and would have laughed at it if they had).

Just for fun, let's come up with a list of things that don't have a long historical tradition of any sort: the bridal bouquet (emerged around the turn of the twentieth century; before that women held prayer books or handkerchiefs), the once-worn formal white dress (became popular in the early to mid-twentieth century thanks to a serious marketing effort), the catered reception (came into vogue in the 1950s), the unity candle (invented in the 1970s as part of a soap opera script). And we could go on and on and on.

The real key is discovering what tradition means to you and to your family. Though women have not been getting married in churches since time immemorial, maybe your mother and your grandmother got married in a church, and perhaps you want to follow in their footsteps. If a tradition means something to you or the people you love, you should pay attention to it. But if it doesn't, ignore it. Unless your religion requires it, it's not mandatory to get married in a church, nor is it particularly historical. You're not thumbing your nose at the order of things if you don't have all the frills of a church wedding (an aisle runner, programs, a wedding party, etc.). Tradition is malleable and varied, and what's important is that you make it yours.

Etiquette Is on the Side of Simplicity

Not only is tradition not quite what you've been led to believe, but etiquette is also a lot less demanding than expected. There is a distinct difference between the dictates of the wedding industry and actual etiquette. There are many lovely people in the wedding industry, but when people who have a financial interest in your impending nuptials give you advice, it's helpful to take that advice with a grain of salt. "Hmm," one might say, "if I follow this advice, will it involve me spending more money? Yes? Well, then does this sound like real tradition, or the kind someone made up?" Because the wedding industry can be a tad self-serving. When a photographer tells you the best way to afford an expensive photographer is to cut your guest list because guests are expensive, it's appropriate to raise an eyebrow. When a bridal magazine tells you it's mandatory to purchase expensive invitations, again, by all means, take a pause.

But the trouble is, faux tradition is more insidious then we even suspect. The catered reception? Not historical at all. So when books and magazines instruct you that it's more proper to have your wedding reception dinner served by waiters in black tie than to have it served buffet style, it can be tricky to remember that every single thing about that sentiment is made up. Even in your mother's day, most people didn't serve a full wedding meal, so etiquette has nothing to say about how this newly mandated meal *should* be served.

What Is Etiquette Anyway, and Is It Stuffy?

Which brings us to etiquette itself: What is it, and how much attention should you pay it?

Let's define etiquette this way: it is about making sure other people's feelings are taken into consideration. It's about graciousness. Think of it as a speed bump on the road to self-absorbed wedding hell. One of the ways to be kind to those around us is to treat our shared cultural history with a healthy sense of respect. This doesn't mean we have to do everything the way it has Always Been Done (since as we've discussed, most things haven't been done that way for very long in the first place). It's about understanding where your granny is coming from, and making allowances for her if you're doing something she'll find disorienting.

Etiquette is not something to be scared of. It's on the side of simplicity and common sense. It is decidedly not on the side of the "Spend more! Personalize it! Make it yours!" wedding culture, and anyone who leads you to believe that it is is lying.

Simplicity Rules

Since you'll hear a lot of made-up etiquette during wedding planning, let's focus on simple and important guidelines. Here are some issues of etiquette that you really should pay attention to (even if you haven't been hearing much about these particular rules):

- On your wedding day, you are a host. Wedding literature seems bent on convincing you that your wedding day is all about *you*. And it is, sort of. You are the one getting married. But whenever you are hosting a party for a lot of your friends and loved ones, it's your responsibility to make sure those people are taken care of. So when making etiquette decisions, try to put the feelings of your guests first, and you'll generally do just fine. Feed your guests on time. Don't force them to wear outfits that match your color scheme. Thank them for attending. Don't boss them around. Treat them like they are people you love, show them that you are honored they will be spending an important day with you. If you do this, I will join etiquette in giving you a delighted thumbs-up.

- Your wedding day should reflect your life as it's lived. No money for gold-plated swans in your day-to-day life?

Well, lucky enough, that means you're off the hook for providing gold-plated swans for your wedding reception (even if the lack of such swans is going to hurt your Aunt Mindy's feelings). Anyone who tries to make you feel guilty about not having a lavish wedding is, in fact, acting in very poor taste.

- Your wedding day should reflect your loved ones as they are. Your mom doesn't need to go on a diet so she looks like someone she's not on your wedding day. Your long-estranged father shouldn't walk you down the aisle. You don't need wedding parties in matching sizes or genders. Etiquette is, after all, about taking the emotions of those you love into consideration, not about mindlessly following a bunch of made-up rules that hurt people's feelings.

- You are allowed to leave out the bouquet toss, etc. There is no rule that you have to collect every wedding tradition that's ever been created and try to cram it into a few hours on your wedding day. If a tradition doesn't mean something to you, you're allowed to let it go. You're not allowed to rub people's faces in the fact that you are the more evolved person, so you're not doing things at your wedding that they did at their wedding. That would be rude, and impolite to boot. But you are allowed to quietly go about creating a ritual that works for you and not spend a minute worrying that you're doing something improper.

- Your wedding is not a show. There is a lot of material out there that would lead you to believe that your wedding is best viewed as a production that should be geared for the maximum entertainment of your guests. It's not, and

most of your guests know better. Your wedding consists
of a ceremony where you make hugely emotional vows
and a party to celebrate that commitment, and that's
more than enough. It doesn't need to be gussied up with
paper goods and lighting and fancy dresses. It can be, but
those things are for fun's sake, not for etiquette's sake.

Reclaiming Traditions

Dealing with (Well-Meaning?) Advice

People like to use words like "etiquette" and "tradition" to boss
you around and to get you to fulfill their vision of what your
wedding should be. When people are trying to push you
around, correct information, casually mentioned, can do wonders. "Actually," you say, "for most of the history of the United
States, people got married at home. So really I'm trying to embrace something traditional in a way that's meaningful to me."

People also use etiquette out of fear. "But we have to do it
this way" can be a code for "I'm afraid my friends will judge me
if we don't." If the person who's afraid of judgment is someone
you love (mothers are particularly prone to the Wedding Judgment Fear), the best thing you can do is talk things out with
her, and find out her real reasons for insisting on XYZ wedding
tradition. Information might help, but what's really going to fix
it is getting to the root of what she's really afraid of, and empowering her with a little "f*ck 'em if they don't like the chairs"
philosophy. Because yes, sometimes moms need to be reminded
that they are allowed to not care what other people think, too.

Remember, planning a wedding is the first step you will
take as part of the process of creating a new family in the eyes of
your community. Part of the (sometimes painful) process
of owning your new role is learning to stand up to people. Gra-
ciously. When people push you around, inform them of what

you're doing and why. Or change the subject. Your wedding is your business, and etiquette holds no truck with bullying.

"Tradition" Is Not a Bad Word

Tradition is what you make of it. When you decide to get married, you are, in a sense, choosing to side with tradition. When we started planning our wedding, we asked my parents if they wanted veto power on any of our decisions, and they told us no. My dad explained, "First, we trust your judgment. Second, with weddings, tradition always wins, because getting married is, in its very essence, traditional. So make whatever choices you want. They'll be traditional enough."

And for me, this is the essence of tradition—a way to sort through a long history of ritual and create something that's meaningful to you. Clare Adama, a theologian who got married in Edinburgh, Scotland, wisely advised, "The Latin origin of tradition, *traditio* means not only to hand on but to hand over, and the meanings of practices such as those within weddings are not rigid, but given on to us to value and interpret in our own contexts." Weddings provide a wonderful opportunity to sit down and discuss with our partners who we are and what we believe. We do ourselves a great disservice when we allow tradition to encompass only the things we are sold instead of the things that have meaning in our hearts. Embrace the aspects of wedding rituals that have meaning to you, and let the rest go. Know that no matter what you choose, you'll be standing on the shoulders of many women who have gone before you.

And as for etiquette, well, if you're being kind and thoughtful, you're probably doing just fine. Be sure to raise an eyebrow at anyone who tells you otherwise.

THE PRACTICAL BRIDE REMEMBERS . . .

- When people tell you about wedding "traditions," be wary. Though the basic outline of weddings has remained relatively unchanged since the 1920s, over the past few decades the size of weddings has drastically increased.

- Figure out what traditions mean something to you and your loved ones, and don't worry about the rest.

- Etiquette is simply about making sure other people's feelings are taken into consideration and can serve as a speed bump on the road to self-absorbed wedding hell.

- Try to realize that the registry isn't about you, or materialism, or even the wedding. It's about letting your guests support you in building a marriage and a life together.

- Here are the basic rules of wedding etiquette: be kind, be thoughtful, be honest, and don't mortgage the farm to pretend you're someone you're not for five hours.

- Weddings are a good time to discuss with our partners what we believe. We do ourselves a great disservice when we allow tradition to encompass only the things we are sold instead of the things that have meaning in our hearts.

4

THE
BUDGET

How Much Does a Wedding Cost?

There are two basic questions you need to consider: How much does a wedding cost? And how much is *my* wedding going to cost? Though it's helpful to get an answer to the first question, try not to get it confused with the answer to the second question. As previously discussed, in the past twenty years or so, the price of weddings in the United States (and the expectation of professionalism at weddings) has gone through the roof. So, when you start researching average wedding budgets in your area, it's easy to become convinced that you will never be able to afford to get married, ever. So, let's just lay this out now: throwing a wedding costs a lot more than it should. That said, you can afford to get married, no matter how much or how little you have to spend. In this chapter we'll discuss researching wedding costs, figuring out who is going to help you pay for the wedding, putting your budget on paper, making the seemingly endless budget decisions, and even making the occasional happy splurge.

A PRACTICAL BRIDE SPEAKS
A Broke-Ass L.A. Wedding
BY DANA LARUE

When we were first engaged, we were overwhelmed. There were so many options, checklist items, possibilities. . . . We didn't know where to start. So we sat down to hammer out what mattered most, and what we could let go. We quickly realized that to us, the wedding wasn't just "an event" or "one day" but a new beginning . . . and we wanted to kick it all off with that in mind.

Oh, and we wanted it to be a balls-out party. Can't leave that out.

As we got closer to the date, our to-do list loomed long and heavy, and I got nervous. Nervous something might go wrong. Something might be forgotten. We had to slash what felt like a zillion projects from the list, and I worried we'd regret it. But then the morning of, I woke up and realized that there was nothing to be nervous about. It was what it was, no changing it now . . . and I just let go. And what it was, was exactly what we needed it to be. I wouldn't change a thing.

As it turns out, I don't even remember most of the things we ended up omitting. Instead, I remember the ceremony that we crafted to reflect our own journey and priorities as a couple. The song our officiant wrote especially for us. Our hands on each other's hearts during the vows. Our friends and family all gathered in our honor. The ring-warming ceremony. The comments

[continues]

from our guests about how original and personal it all was. Dancing with my dad. Getting dipped by my husband. Laughter. Hugs. Tears. Mojitos. Dancing. Saying "I do." Kissing a lot.

And of course it wasn't all perfection. I forgot my bouquet when I walked down the aisle. (Didn't faze me.) I ripped a huge hole in my dress while stomping the glass and had to cut two inches off my skirt at the reception. (Makes a great story.) I sprained my ankle getting "too low" on the dance floor, got up and kept dancing, and spent our honeymoon on crutches. But I love these memories. They made our wedding even more authentic and organic. We're messy and imperfect and real . . . and I love that our wedding reflected that, too.

So don't worry that people will think you're cheap if you DIY your own flowers, omit the favors, iPod your dance floor, or whatever the corners you cut may be. Don't fret about what they'll think, whether you want to be married by a pastor or a pagan queen. Your guests are there to celebrate you and your love. Not to criticize your chair selection. And if they do, f*ck 'em.

And don't worry about everything being perfect. What does that even mean, anyway? What's really perfect is getting married at your own wedding. So just focus on that, and you'll be just fine. The rest, as they say, is cake! My best advice? Just have fun.

Don't get pressured by expectation or tradition if that's not your thing.

Don't feel you have to be über-original, if tradition suits your fancy as a couple.

Don't be pressured to have a million perfectly coordinated details.

Don't confuse "expensive" with "better."

And don't let self-consciousness impede your enjoyment.

Do honor your partner's wishes and include them in decision-making.

Do just be your wonderful selves, and let the day reflect that.

Do surrender to the joy, breathe in the bliss, and let go.

Do say please and thank you a lot (it's simple, but so true).

And again, do have fun.

Do Your Research (It's Scary but Necessary)

There is a reason to research average wedding prices, scary as they are. If you're not experienced at throwing events, you just don't know what they cost. And because reality matters, you need to establish a framework before you start making plans. If the average catering cost in your area is $10,000, and you have $5,000 to spend on food, it's good to know that you will probably need to get creative and make some compromises. Maybe you'll do your research and hire an up-and-comer, or maybe you'll have a breakfast wedding. But chances are, you're not going to get the most popular joint in town for a Saturday night lobster dinner, and the sooner you realize that, the happier you'll be.

Figure Out What You Want to Spend

Once you've researched average wedding costs in your area, you're ready to figure out what your wedding will cost. Here is the most important part: trust yourself. Marie-Ève Laforte, who married in an apple orchard outside Montreal, said, "Don't listen when anyone tells you that you simply have to spend this and that much on something. You really don't. In fact, you don't have to do anything that does not feel right to you, or that makes you feel financially uncomfortable." If the cost of something feels unsettling, chances are, you shouldn't do it. Let it go. Move on and look for other options. If you're willing to compromise and be creative (not to mention ruthlessly cut things from your budget that you don't care about), you absolutely will be able to find a solution that lets you sleep at night.

Putting It on Paper

When it comes to the nitty-gritty of building your wedding budget, figure out (a) what kind of wedding you want (see exercises in Chapter 1), and (b) exactly how much money you have to spend.

Not Everything Is Equally Important

What's important to you? In Chapter 1, you and your partner worked to make a list of your wedding priorities. Now it's time to translate these priorities into a real-life spending plan. Make two lists: things you want to put more resources toward, and things you want to put fewer resources toward. Be ruthless. Sure, everyone says you have to have wedding flowers, but if you don't want to spend much on flowers, put them on the "fewer resources" list. This doesn't mean you won't have flowers or you won't spend any money on flowers. It just means that you're deprioritizing flower spending. Maybe you'll have fake flowers, or maybe you'll use grocery store flowers that your maid of honor arranged for you day-of. But mostly you're not going to worry too much about flowers when you're building your budget. Think of it this way: it's better to do a few things well than to do a lot of things poorly. If you go to a wedding with a great bluegrass band and potluck food, you're just going to remember how much fun you had dancing, not that they didn't have fancy food. So put your money toward a few items that are worth it to you, and don't worry too much about the rest.

But try to avoid falling into the trap of thinking that how much you spend on something indicates how much you care about it. Sometimes items that didn't top your priority list end up being things you spend more on. There will be times in wedding planning when you think, "I do not care about this thing, and I will rip out my eyes if I have to think about it for one more second. Hence, I will throw money at it." Or as Kimberly Eclipse, who married in Long Island, New York, said, "Sometimes money is just numbers on paper. If there was something that we really wanted, or felt that we needed to do, then we paid for it. No, I didn't want to go above a certain amount, but that arbitrary amount became less important than what it paid for." There are also times you'll want to pay money to make a problem go away.

And sometimes the things you care the most about are those that cost the least: a dress you made yourself, the toasts people will make around the table, the time you spent with your mom putting together your flowers. Sometimes *how* we spend our money is more important than *how much of it* we spend. So if you buy affordable fabric to make your wedding dress with your mom but then throw $1,000 at hiring a day-of coordinator so you don't ever have to think about logistics again, that's a sane choice.

Budgeting Tricks

When building your budget, I recommend stealing tips from the event-planning pros. For example, know that all events go over budget, almost without exception. The way to go over budget without causing injury to life, limb, or your credit score is to plan for it. Karen Palmer, who married in Burlington, Vermont, and also happens to plan events for a living, suggested budgeting in a "slush fund" line that is 10–15 percent of your total budget. This money is not to be touched except in case of emergencies, which might mean booking the DJ you fell in love with, or could mean true, last-minute, the-caterer-canceled emergencies. If a slush fund doesn't make sense for you (or your budget isn't quite that organized), it might be helpful to think in terms of a target budget and a maximum budget. Maybe you really want to spend $20,000, but you know that if it comes down to it, you can spend $24,000. Aim for the lower number, and if you hit the higher number instead, no harm, no foul (and no guilt).

Another tip worth stealing is deceptively simple: include *everything* in your budget. When looking at the massive sum of money you're going to spend on your wedding, it's easy to start telling yourself little lies. Lies like "invitations don't cost that much; we don't really need to include them" or "postage—that's a totally negligible expense." Stephanie Marienau Turpin, who had a joyful wedding in Washington, D.C., said, "It was really powerful for my then-fiancé and I to list out everything we would need to spend on related to the wedding, not just the ceremony and reception. Including all those things certainly made our final number bigger than we wanted to see, but not accounting for those costs at the beginning of planning would have led to more trouble." I'm not suggesting that you make yourself crazy trying to think of every two-dollar expenditure you have to make, but a lot of negligible expenses will add up to a sizable expense. The more things you can count, the more realistic your budget will be.

No, You Don't Have to Add It Up

Or you can take the exact opposite tack, and add nothing up. The trouble with wedding budgets is they can take on an emotional life of their own. Spend enough time reading about reasonably priced weddings, and you'll start tying your pride to your budget number. You'll think, "I'm having a $10,000 wedding, damn it, and not a penny more," and then the week before the wedding when you figure out that you have $2,000 in plane ticket expenses that you didn't see coming, you'll find yourself a sobbing mess on the floor as you try to explain to your partner that you had a budget number in mind, and what are you going to do now that you're over that budget?

So, in these moments of temporary insanity, it's important to remember that you're not reporting your final budget to anyone.

You're not publishing it on the Internet, you're not passing it out to your friends, you're not telling total strangers. What you spend is your business, and after the wedding is over, you're going to find out it doesn't matter very much. So add it up creatively if it makes you feel better. Or don't add it up at all.

Or heck, don't have a budget in the first place. Kirsten Duke, who got married on her neighbor's property in Ontario, Canada, found that "not having a budget kept me sane. I got an influx of cash in December, so we started planning around that. From that point, we spent money on the wedding whenever we had extra out of our paychecks, and from gifts from our parents and grandparents. I honestly to this day have no idea what we spent. I have an approximate idea, but in the end the system that worked best for us was to just continually move forward."

Real Wedding Budgets

I'm not going to give you one of those percentage budget breakdowns (i.e., expect to spend 12 percent of your budget on a photographer), because there are as many ways to handle a budget as there are people. The following pages feature a range of budgets that allow you to think about what might work for you. There is a $5,000 civil ceremony wedding; a $15,000 big-city wedding where the couple spent almost nothing on their delicious food; a $13,000 wedding in a more affordable part of the country, with a full, seated dinner for 150 people; and a $35,000 destination wedding where the couple splurged on renting a house where everyone could spend the weekend together. I hope this serves as something of a springboard for creative wedding thinking. Money is just the starting point for making a thoughtful plan that works for you.

[continues]

$5,000, CHICAGO, ILLINOIS • Ashley and Zach LaMotte got married in a simple civil ceremony in Chicago, followed by a restaurant lunch with lots of wine and cheer with friends and family. They splurged a bit on their outfits, as well as on rings, because they are going to wear those rings for a lifetime. That, and they went on a Mediterranean cruise for their honeymoon, which seems like an excellent way to spend money!

INVITATIONS: $25
Made by the bride, using materials she had on hand.

RECEPTION: $1,000
Lunch for twenty-two at a restaurant, including lots of wine, dessert, and tip.

WEDDING LICENSE AND VENUE: $50
The Chicago Cultural Center, where the City of Chicago performs civil ceremonies on Saturday mornings (and you're allowed to bring twenty or so people to cheer you on!).

PHOTOGRAPHER: $250
Two hours of coverage.

FLOWERS: $0
The bride and her mom made the bouquet and her husband's boutonniere out of vintage fabric flowers they already owned.

DRESS: $1,082
A splurge! She fell in love with the dress and later sold it for $500. Ashley said, "I loved that dress every dollar of that $1,082, and I love the dishwasher we bought with the $500 we got when we sold it, too."

SUIT AND HAT: $375
A three-piece suit and a hat that the groom loves and has worn multiple times since the wedding.

[continues]

WEDDING RINGS: $2,100
Why not splurge a little? They'll wear them for a lifetime.

$15,000, SAN FRANCISCO, CALIFORNIA · Steffany Farros planned a $15,000 wedding for seventy-five people in San Francisco, which is tough in a city where the average wedding costs double that. So she threw out convention and came up with a plan that worked for her. The wedding ceremony took place at city hall, with the reception at an up-and-coming nightclub, and catering by the best taco truck in the city. This gave the couple an intimate ceremony, a raging dance party, and delicious food that cost almost nothing. Also, they splurged on good photography and a photo booth because they decided that mattered to them.

CITY HALL MARRIAGE LICENSE: $100

CITY HALL CEREMONY FEE: $72

CITY HALL PHOTOGRAPHY: $500

VENUE: $5,891
Included rental for nine hours, four hours of open bar with good booze, all taxes, and use of all audiovisual equipment. The couple asked two friends to DJ.

CATERING: $920
A taco truck, three hours of service.
Cupcakes: eight dozen from a local bakery.

SAVE-THE-DATES: $25
One hundred, ordered through an online printer.

INVITATIONS: $220
Custom comic-book invites.

[continues]

THANK-YOU CARDS: $25
Sixty, ordered through an online printer.

FLOWERS: $250
Made by the bride and her bridal brigade, with flowers from the San Francisco Flower Mart.

TABLE/LINEN/CHAIR RENTAL: $138
Three tables seating ten from a party rental company. Since the venue was a club, it had some seating already.

PHOTOGRAPHY: $3,470

PHOTO BOOTH: $1,150

RINGS: $1,100

CLOTHES: $1,030
The dress cost $780 and was made by an independent designer. The groom's clothing budget was $250.

$13,000, COLUMBUS, OHIO · Becky Leach-Seymour and Matthew Seymour got married in Columbus, Ohio, with a $13,000 budget, and 150 guests (double the number of guests that Steffany had in San Francisco). But Columbus is a much less expensive area, so they were able to have more formal wedding for a similar cost.

ATTIRE, HAIR, AND MAKEUP FOR BRIDE AND GROOM: $1,400
The dress was a splurge at $900 from a local boutique. The groom wore a rented tuxedo.

CEREMONY AND WEDDING LICENSE: $540
The Catholic church had a mandatory $500 donation for the ceremony, and the Ohio wedding license was $40.

[continues]

RECEPTION: $7,000
Venue rental, sit-down dinner, and open beer and wine bar for 150 guests.

INVITATIONS AND STATIONERY: $350
Custom invitations designed by a friend and printed through an online service. Programs and save-the-dates made by the bride.

FLOWERS AND RECEPTION DECOR: $1,000
Bouquets, boutonnieres, and corsages were made by the bride and bridesmaids with the help of a local florist. Centerpieces and reception decor were a collection of mismatched lanterns, mostly from IKEA.

CEREMONY AND RECEPTION MUSIC: $770
$150 each for the church organist and vocalist; $470 for a DJ for five hours.

ATTENDANT GIFTS: $350

PHOTOGRAPHY: $1,200
Two shooters for eight hours.

DIY PHOTO BOOTH: $300

$35,000, SMALL-TOWN MAINE • Christine and Curtis Smith got married in Bethel, Maine, a ski resort town. They married during the off-season of summer but splurged on renting a private home for a whole week (the wedding and the honeymoon rolled into one!) to house their bridal party and families, as well as to serve as the venue for their sixty-person wedding. They also paid for a delicious lobster rehearsal dinner. The couple wanted a way to spend some quality time with their friends and family, so their wedding allowed them a full weekend to bond with their loved ones. And what the heck! The couple married in their late thirties and paid for the wedding almost entirely on their own, so why not create an unconventional wedding that really worked for them?

[continues]

LOBSTER REHEARSAL DINNER: $3,000

A traditional New England lobster bake for all sixty guests, including rentals, linens, some basic decorations, and limited alcohol (beer and sangria).

VENUE: $11,000

A private home rented for the week, where family and friends could stay and the couple could honeymoon.

CATERING: $3,700

Included a family-style dinner with three entrée choices and appetizers for both a preceremony celebration (guests were shuttled to the venue) and traditional cocktail hour.

ALCOHOL: $2,500

A definite splurge on quality wine and top-shelf liquor. Alcohol was self-supplied but a bartender was hired to serve.

CAKE: $175

No traditional cake here. Individual chocolate lava cakes were purchased from an acquaintance's daughter, a recent pastry school graduate.

RENTALS: $2,000

Included thirteen tables, sixty Chiavari chairs, linens, place settings, glassware, serving platters, and fee for delivery.

OFFICIANT: $0

The bride's good friend officiated the service.

INVITATIONS: $200

Do-it-yourself via Paper Source.

WEDDING RINGS: $2,300

DRESS: $1,800

The wedding dress was $1,250; she spent $550 on accessories and alterations.

[continues]

GROOM'S ATTIRE: $400
A new suit for the groom along with a pair of expensive shoes.

MAKEUP AND HAIR: $300
Hair was a gift from the bride's close friend, and she also hired an airbrush makeup artist.

FLOWERS: $1,000
This included bouquets for the bride and six bridesmaids, eight boutonnieres, six centerpieces, and two very large ceremony arrangements.

DECORATIONS: $500
Candles, candles, and more candles.

MUSIC: $1,400
Total of eight hours of music from a DJ, for both ceremony and reception.

TRANSPORTATION: $250
Shuttle transportation to and from the wedding for guests not staying in the house.

WEDDING-PARTY GIFTS: $1,800
Suits, shirts, and cuff links for the guys; Tiffany necklaces and Coach wristlets for the ladies.

PHOTOGRAPHER: $2,600
Eight hours of coverage, two photographers, and no albums. Also included one night's lodging for photographers.

If you tend to operate in a more freewheeling fashion, or if a wedding budget is going to make you OCD insane, it's perfectly responsible to just try to spend an amount that feels sensible to you on each item. You're two fully grown adults. You absolutely can throw a wedding with no formal budget but with a lot of common sense.

Who Pays? (And What Does That Mean?)

There are as many different configurations of people paying for a wedding as there are families. Your first step is to figure out whether you want to ask loved ones to help contribute to your wedding funds. Keep in mind people who contribute money are going to feel that they have a legitimate involvement in the project that is your wedding. Though it's up to you to set boundaries on what that level of involvement will be, the first thing to consider is whom you want involved in the first place. If you have a difficult relationship with your family, or if you want to call all the shots yourself, let that influence your decision.

You may also find yourself in a situation where you have family who very much want to contribute and participate in wedding planning but simply can't afford to chip in financially. In that case, we'll talk about ways for you to let them feel involved, because even though this chapter is all about budgets, money isn't everything.

Your Family Is Helping to Pay

Talking to Your Family

Before you walk into a conversation with your family about contributing financially to the wedding, make sure you have a pretty good idea of what kind of wedding you're throwing (at least tentatively). It's not fair to ask your parents to help pay for what they think is a Catholic Mass wedding, only to surprise them with the barefoot-in-a-meadow plan after they've written a check. Have several long talks with your partner and do your research so you are prepared for the talk with your family. A fair conversation is one that starts with the facts. "We're thinking of doing a secular wedding service followed by a lunch reception. We think the price will be somewhere between $10,000 and $25,000, depending on the location and the length of the guest list. Let's talk about what your preferences are, and then you can think about how much (and if) you'd like to contribute financially."

Next up, you need to talk about how much your parents can contribute—realistically. Remember, by this point in the process, you've gotten a good idea of what weddings cost, and your parents may have no idea (and if they're assuming wedding costs are comparable to those of twenty years ago, they might end up shell-shocked). So lay out your projection of expenses, and then let them think it over.

Then talk specific numbers. Money is hard to talk about, so it's easy to get sucked into the land of vague. "Sure," they say, "we'll pay for the venue, within reason." It may be hard to nail down real numbers now, but it's going to be a lot more awkward telling them you just booked a venue that costs three times what they expected to pay. While you're asking difficult questions, find out when your parents' money will arrive. Maybe they can hand you a check right away. Maybe they can hand you a check the day before the wedding. Though you should be grateful in both circumstances, they represent very different cash management strategies, so make sure you know the plan up front.

And here is the kicker: make sure they are offering you money that they can afford to contribute. A bride's parents in particular sometimes have an emotional need to pay for their daughter's wedding. This may lead to parents offering cash that they really need for retirement or bills, which is no good. The same rule that holds true for your wedding spending holds true for your parents' wedding spending: if it doesn't feel right, it probably isn't. And no one should cash out her retirement for a party . . . even a really nice, very important party.

Ways for People to Contribute

If one or both of your families are helping to pay for your wedding (or heck, totally paying for your wedding), there are a number of ways to handle contributions that feel fair.

The even split: It may be sensible to split your wedding budget evenly among contributors. We split our wedding budget into fourths: my parents paid for 25 percent, my husband's parents paid for 25 percent, and each of us paid for another 25 percent from our savings. There are as many ways to divide budgets as there are families, but the even split has the advantage of making everyone feel like an equal contributor. Also, it prevents any one person from feeling like he or she can call the shots.

Based on timing: Think of this as the cash-flow solution to the problem. If one party has access to money now (say, your parents) and another party is still saving to help pay for the wedding (say, you), you can divide payment by timing. Your parents pay for all the up-front costs, like deposits, and you pay for all the late-in-the-game costs, like catering.

Based on interest: It may be that your parents really care what wedding venue you end up with, or what food you serve. In that case, they may want to pay for your venue and food. Or maybe they don't have a whole lot of cash to contribute, but your mom really wants to buy your dress. In this case, it might make sense to divide up the wedding budget by item. Be aware, however, that if your parents are paying for a specific item, they will probably expect to have a say on that aspect of the wedding.

From each, according to ability: Perhaps what feels fair to you is having people give according to what they've got. If your husband's parents are well off and your parents are struggling, $5,000 from your parents may be as meaningful as $50,000 from his family. If you take this route, it might be wise to keep each person's contribution private. "She gave a meaningful amount" is all anyone needs to know.

Setting Planning Boundaries

Though it's important to know what kind of wedding you might want before the conversation with your parents, it's also important to be ready to listen to what your parents want (which we discuss in more detail in Chapter 1). But establish from the get-go that money does not buy influence and that everyone is in this project together.

Establish boundaries and expectations for wedding planning early. If you want your mom to go with you to every vendor meeting and help you agonize over colors, tell her now. If you are going to make some decisions without the influence of your parents, be up front about it. People who are sinking large sums of cash into your wedding will, understandably, care about the process, and you should tell them what to expect.

It's also important to respect your families' contributions, no matter how you plan the party. The money your parents are putting into the wedding is money they worked hard for, and money they could be spending on a nice vacation or on paying down their mortgage. Treat it with the same respect that you would your own hard-earned money.

Oh, the Guilt

Once your family has offered money, your job is to accept it with a healthy mix of love and gratitude. It's easy to get sucked into the guilt of accepting money and to lose track of the fact that your wedding is an important milestone, in which your family wants to be involved and to show their love and support for you. For them, that might mean writing you a check. Katie Pegher told me that when she was worrying for the millionth time in the planning process over the money they were being given, her fiancé's stepmother "threw the paperwork on the dashboard and looked me square in the eye. 'I make a damn good living,' she said, 'and I *want* to do this.'" So as hard as it can be to accept money, let it go. Your wedding is not all about you, and if you don't personally earn every penny that's spent on it, that's just fine.

You Are Paying

Perhaps you're paying for your wedding on your own. Maybe you feel terrified by the responsibility. Maybe you feel relieved that you're in control. Regardless, realize how empowering this is. You're doing this on your own, and that is worth celebrating.

The advantage to paying for a wedding on your own is clear: you get to kindly outvote pushy family members. But there is a catch: your family might not be helping you pay, but they may really want to be involved in your wedding. So ask them to participate in a way that's meaningful to them. Maybe your mom comes wedding-dress shopping with you, maybe she makes the programs, or maybe she just holds your hand as you freak out before you walk down the aisle. But just like paying for a wedding doesn't equal control over a wedding, not paying for a wedding doesn't negate involvement. Even if she didn't pay for a dollar of the party, chances are that your mom still wants to be your mom as you wend your way through this important life transition.

Sane Budget Rules

Once you have your wedding budget set, you've moved past theory and into practice. And practice is tricky. With that in mind, here are some rules for wedding decision-making that will keep you reasonably sane (considering).

As little Wedding Think as you can manage: The wedding industry loves to perpetuate the idea that it's your "one big day," and you deserve it, whatever "it" is. It's easy to get sucked into the trap of buying $500 shoes because you start to feel like it won't make that big of a difference to the budget anyway. Then you get a dress that is double what you were going to spend, because it's just so pretty. Then your venue is triple what you expected . . . and suddenly you're stuck with a budget you can't possibly afford. So although you shouldn't nickel-and-dime every silly purchase, and you probably will make a few splurges, watch to make sure the "but we deserve it" line of thinking isn't sneaking into big-ticket items.

No guilt: All that said, trust yourself. You decided on a budget that you can afford, and dang it, you are going to let yourself spend that money without guilting yourself every step of the way. You're lucky enough to have a chunk of money to put into the economy and to support businesses and artisans whose work you value. That's a blessing, so stop wasting your energy on guilt.

No second-guessing: Once you make a financial decision that feels right to you, stick to your guns. Wedding planning can be a constant pattern of questioning your own judgment, and this will drive you mad. If your choice was right for you, that's it. You're done, and you're fine.

Yes, Paying for a Wedding Sucks

There. It needed to be said. Weddings are expensive. Arguably, weddings are *too* expensive these days, no matter how you slice them. And while you're in the middle of it, writing check after check after check, it can feel abjectly terrible. If you find yourself thinking, "Why are we doing this?" and "Is it going to be worth it?" and "Maybe we should just elope so we don't have to pay these bills," over and over again, know that you're in the best kind of company.

In the end, if you spend an amount of money that felt reasonable to you (back when you were deciding on your budget, you were probably in a far saner mood than you are now), it will probably feel worth it in the end. And even if it doesn't, it will have the remarkable advantage of being over. The money will be spent, the wedding will be a joyful day in your memory, and you'll realize that you never have to spend that money ever again. And that will feel like freedom.

Somehow, Everything Is Possible

If you have a limited budget, you're going to hear a lot of "can't" and "won't be able to." But so much more is possible than you imagine. People have been having weddings with not a lot of money since time immemorial. Once you've said yes to having a wedding, it's your job to say yes to the people around you who want to help. Stop listening to the people who tell you no, and start paying attention when people tell you yes. Your best friend wants to make you a wedding cake? Yes! Your parents' church will let you use the social hall for free? Yes! Your sister will loan you her wedding dress? Yes! A nonprofessional cake can be tasty, and you can make a church social hall look cute, and your wedding dress can be meaningful *and* stylish. You will be able to make your wedding what you need it to be with the elements you have available to you.

There Are No Pockets in a Shroud

In the depths of planning, weddings can feel like they are about money, but they are not. Weddings are about love, about family, and about a major life transition. They're also about things like logistics, and enjoying yourself. And sometimes that costs money, and that's worth it. Jen Smith summed it up well when she said, "Peace of mind isn't a splurge. Color-coordinated, choreographed doves that launch fireworks are a splurge. Depending on your priorities, hiring a DJ might be a splurge or it might be the most important purchase; only you will know." So, when you realize that getting a DJ will make the party for you, or that those expensive red shoes will give you a feeling of explosive joy? Sometimes it's worth it to just do it.

The amount of money you spend on your wedding doesn't have a deeper meaning. It doesn't make you a better person. It's just a number. It's just dollar bills. And even your granny will tell you, there are no pockets in a shroud. You're getting married, damn it. So, even with your sensible budget, try to enjoy the heck out of that (even if that means you splurge a little on those joyful red shoes).

THE PRACTICAL BRIDE REMEMBERS . . .

- Research average wedding prices in your area, and then think about what you want to spend. These numbers do not have to be the same.
- Prioritize your spending: What do you want to put money toward? Feel empowered to ruthlessly cut other budget items.
- If you're accepting money from your families to help pay for the wedding, be clear up front on how you're splitting payment, actual budget numbers, and what your wedding planning boundaries are.
- If you and your partner are paying for the wedding yourselves, remember to take a moment to celebrate how empowering that is.
- Once you've set your budget, acknowledge that although paying for a wedding can really suck, there is no reason to guilt yourself or second-guess your decisions.
- Focus on all the times you hear yes during wedding planning. Making a joyful wedding happen on a limited budget is eminently doable. Don't let people tell you otherwise.
- Remember, in the end, weddings are not about money. If you splurge here and there on things that make you happy? Well, no pockets in a shroud.

wedding planning is as much about decision-making as it is about style (though we're going to discuss the beautiful stuff, too).

Know Thyself and Be Thyself

To survive wedding planning, you need to find a way to embrace your basic nature. Desaray Evans, who married in a Quaker ceremony outside of Washington, D.C., told me, "At some point in the process, I realized that planning a wedding wasn't going to change fundamental aspects of my personality. I was not suddenly going to become highly motivated, detail-oriented, budget-conscious, or crafty." As much as we hope that the day we start wedding planning is the day we wake up as a crafty stylist, chances are, it's not going to happen. The sooner you own up to this, the better off you'll be.

You're a pretty fantastic person just the way you are (that's why someone is committing to you for life). So take a second to think about what you're good at, and what is not your bag. When you're throwing a party in your regular life, what are your strengths and weaknesses? What parts are you brilliant at? The food? Decorating? Selecting the right group of people? Throwing together an informal party quickly? What parts are you terrible at? I'm good at motivating people to come to our parties, and my husband is excellent at serving the right food and drink, but we're both lousy at decorating. When we're throwing a party, I always have vague stylish ideas: "We'll get tons of black and silver balloons, and then fill the apartment with them." But I'm fundamentally lazy at execution: "Oops! Can I get balloons in twenty-four hours? Maybe, but that sounds hard. Oh well, balloons are overrated." Given this, it is no great surprise that our wedding had great people and great food, but at the last minute I gave up on more ambitious decorating plans. Think of your wedding as a dolled-up version of the parties you normally throw. That will give you permission to play and get fancy but will help you set realistic expectations.

A PRACTICAL BRIDE SPEAKS
A Wedding Where the People Mattered
BY JAMIE FERGERSON

Early in our relationship, Max and I did not know whether we ever wanted to be married. After we decided to get married, we didn't know whether we wanted a wedding. When we decided to have a wedding, we wanted very different things. Max wanted to grab a few of our loved ones and head to Vegas, while I wanted to have an intimate and nontraditional celebration in the woods. The wedding we had was nothing like either of our original visions, but it somehow became exactly the celebration we needed.

One of the reasons we were originally hesitant to plan a wedding was that I am a perfectionist. I am a perfectionist who has extreme tendencies toward anxiety and hates nothing more than being wrong, and Max and I both knew that wedding planning was likely to push all of my anxious buttons. And it's true that I did worry endlessly throughout our planning about everything from whether our ceremony would be too traditional for our friends or too nontraditional for our families, to whether the kitchen would be able to accommodate all our loved ones' dietary needs, to whether people would think we were cheap for only having a beer and wine bar.

As a sanity-saving measure, though, we decided to try very hard to put most of our worries and our money into the things that mattered most to us: the people, the pictures, and the food. It was a good plan that we executed imperfectly, but when we remember our wedding, these are definitely the three choices about which we are most happy. And the only choice that really matters now is the people who were involved in our wedding.

Max and I both agree that our choice of officiants was the best decision we made in our wedding. We asked two friends—members of our chosen family—to marry us. They have known us and loved us from the beginning of our relationship, and it only seemed right to have them bless us as we moved forward. Having our friends marry us also served as a way to honor our queer and radical community. They are an amazing couple who, despite the fact that they cannot legally marry, model for us all the qualities we'd like to see in our own marriage.

[continues]

But just as the greatest joys in our wedding were because of people, so were the greatest disappointments. About two months before our wedding, someone to whom I had been very close wrote a letter to me explaining all of his objections to our queer union and his disapproval of our marriage. It was the most hurtful thing I've ever read, and I cried for weeks over it. I was unsure until the day of the wedding about whether he would attend, and he chose not to. For a few moments on our wedding day, I felt the pain of that rejection, but it also compelled me to be even more grateful for those friends and family who have offered their support of us and our relationship and were there in either body or spirit.

I find it hard to offer wedding planning advice when I look back on our wedding, because it feels like so little of what we did during our eighteen months of wedding planning mattered. The dress I never wanted to wear and the tablecloths I hated don't matter a bit to me now. Whatever else we got wrong or left undone while planning a wedding, we got the people right, and that is all that matters.

This is also a great time to examine where you need help. If you're terrible at organization (which we'll discuss in greater depth in Chapter 9) and are having a big wedding, now might be the time to ask a friend to help or to hire a (sane) wedding planner. (Trust me, a big wedding is a big undertaking. Don't lie to yourself on that front.) If you're terrible at cooking, for goodness' sake, hire a caterer. The bottom line is, we can't always do it all, and we don't need to.

Edit, Edit, Edit

Here is the deep, dark secret of wedding planning: not everything matters. Trying to do everything will turn you into a crazy person. Brandi Hassouna, who married in a friend's home in Los Angeles, put it this way: "Just the thought of most of the details I initially wanted left me wrung out. I just couldn't do it. My architect fiancé stepped in when he saw me slowly tearing my hair out and suggested we do what all creatives do: edit, edit, edit . . . and then edit a bit more. The house became the color palette. We added a few lanterns with battery-powered LEDs, some pom-poms, a few flower arrangements, and ta-da, the house was ready for a party." Wedding planning has a way of making every small detail seem important, but you can't split your focus between every single detail. So take a moment to re-focus yourself. Go back to the list you made in Chapter 1, look at what you really care about, and allow that to shape which details you will focus on. You might need to have chairs, but unless you put them on the list when you started planning, you don't have to care about what the chairs look like.

Making Decisions ("The Best Is the Enemy of the Good")

Modern wedding planning has a way of immobilizing you, making decisions impossible. When you have tons of options, even the smallest details have a way of seeming very important. Because of the way the human brain works, the more choices we have, the more we are both frozen with indecision and ultimately unhappy with our choice. We're terrified that we will choose incorrectly.

So remember, each choice gets you a step closer to getting married, and nothing is a life-or-death decision, no matter how it feels. I made my most sane wedding decisions the week before the wedding because I didn't have time to dither. I would look at two options, give myself five seconds to think about which one seemed best for us, and go with it. This sort of rapid-fire gut check is a profoundly helpful way to approach the million decisions you need to make during wedding planning. Sure, your gut might not always be right, but in the end, the little decisions won't matter much anyway, so you might as well not waste tons of emotional energy making them. That said, Christen Karle Muir, who married in an old Catholic church in a coastal Northern California town, told me, "Trust your gut, yes, but know that it is okay if your gut has no idea. The most important thing is being okay with your decision, no matter what, after the fact." Make choices you can live with, and then move on. Hopefully, you've picked a good partner to marry, and the rest of your choices will become details.

When it comes to making individual wedding decisions, to quote Voltaire, "The best is the enemy of the good." In other words, good is sometimes good enough, and our endless quest for perfection often ends with us sacrificing good options while we look for the elusive best option. If we wait and wait to pick a wedding vendor because we're not sure whether the ones we have found are quite right, all the good vendors might end up booked before we bite the bullet. So gather your nerve and choose. I can guarantee you that you won't make perfect choices. But I can also guarantee that if you try to make choices that feel right to you and make you happy, they will usually be good enough. And it turns out, the sum of lots of things that are good enough is actually pretty great.

More Decisions (Yes, They Keep Coming): Vendors, the Wedding Party, and More

Now that we've discussed some less crazy ways to make decisions (not everything matters, the best is the enemy of the good, just choose already), let's talk about some of the bigger decisions you are likely to make. Hiring vendors and signing contracts is something you want to go into with your head screwed on straight, because you should be fond of anyone to whom you give a small pile of money. Then there are the personal decisions, like deciding whether you want a wedding party, then picking your wedding party, and making peace with the wedding party you've got. And finally, you'll need to make decisions about all of those pesky tangentially wedding-related bashes. Do you need them? (No.) Do you want them? (Maybe.) Can you make them into something that makes sense for you? (Yes.)

The Six Stages of Wedding Planning

BY KAYCE HAZELGROVE
OF SHINYPRETTYBITS.COM AND FOODIEWASHERE.COM

The progression of states are:

1. EUPHORIA: "SQUEEE"
Usually marked by extreme moments of giddiness and joy. People may remark that you spend inordinate amounts of time staring off into space, smiling like an idiot. It is not unusual to be overcome with the need to run around in circles and shout things like wooo! at the top of your lungs. Minor annoyances like dirty socks on the counter or a toilet seat left up fade under the overwhelming rosy glow of rightness. You may believe you can fly.

2. DISCOVERY: "OOOOH, PRETTY"
Usually coincides with the purchase of wedding magazines or the finding of fancy wedding blogs. Marked by an obsessive attention to detail. Feelings of grandeur may cause you to believe yourself capable of feats you otherwise would never attempt, such as crafting, cooking a meal to feed one hundred–plus people, making bouquets. A person in this stage is usually easy to spot through the use of language, particularly words like Chiavari, bunting flags, letterpress, and STD. It is not uncommon for this stage to precede the first.

[continues]

3. PANIC: "HOW THE HELL?"

Left with the reality of putting plans into action, you may be overwhelmed with the amount of things to do. Cycles of hyperactive crafting and list-making followed by sleeplessness are not uncommon. You may be tempted to run off and elope. Partners may remark on your shorter than normal temper.

This stage often coincides with the first talk of budgets.

4. OUTRAGE/DEPRESSION: "WHAT THE *EFF*," "*EFF* ME"

This stage is marked by feelings of bitterness and frustration. You may feel as though you are failing in some way. This can cause you to swing between feeling angry over all the expectations being placed on you and despondent over your inability to live up. You may find yourself resenting others with friends and family who own a barn, can DJ, or have the enviable ability to craft masterpieces out of bits of random fabric and paper.

5. REBELLION: "*EFF* IT"

Faced with the need to simplify and regain a sense of control, you may start ruthlessly slashing things from the wedding you previously deemed very important. This stage is marked by feelings of apathy and exhaustion. It is not uncommon to find yourself telling overzealous friends and family where to stick their "helpful suggestions." Rebellion can give you a false sense of Zen, resulting in a regression to stage 4. It helps to mock the wedding industry in this phase.

6. ZEN: "IT IS WHAT IT IS"

Having progressed through the other five stages, you are left with a feeling of having done all you could do. Calmness sets in. You accept that things will go wrong but understand that they won't take away from the beauty of the day. This stage is often followed by the drinking of copious amounts of alcohol and the shaking of your bottom.

Hiring Vendors

When it comes to making choices, some of the most expensive decisions you make will be picking your wedding vendors. (Should you choose to have wedding vendors. We'll talk about DIY in Chapter 6.) Right up front, I want to free you from the burden of doing endless research in your quest to somehow hire the perfect vendors (there are no perfect vendors). You should focus your search on finding people you think are sane, and people you personally mesh with. In five years, the wedding photography trends will have changed, but you'll still have memories of the photographer who followed you everywhere on your wedding day, and you want those memories to be genuinely happy, not hilariously horrifying.

This is a good point at which to remind you why your vendor choices matter. Your photographer, should you choose to have one, will be following you around like your personal paparazzo (lying on the ground next to you to get a shot during your first dance). Your venue and caterer will be in charge of making sure things go smoothly (that the doors are unlocked and the tables and food are set up). And your officiant will take on the monumental task of binding you to another person for life (hopefully with a minimum of awkward jokes and banter). And although there is no perfect, there is definitely totally imperfect, so you should listen to your gut when you're choosing whom to hire. The officiant who makes slightly sexist jokes during your interview? Probably not the ideal candidate. The wedding photographer the Internet says is a must-hire but who doesn't promptly return your calls and makes you feel not cool enough over tea? Skip 'im.

When you can, find people whose philosophy you agree with and who make you laugh. When you can't, find people who seem relatively unobjectionable and don't raise any red flags. And feel free to be very clear about expressing your needs and wants. We did not want photographers in our face during our religious service, nor did we want them bossing our guests around during the reception (we'd seen both happen at other weddings). Being really explicit about this in vendor interviews helped us find exactly the right photographers to work with. Because at the end of the day, beautiful wedding pictures are great, but a wedding photographer who makes you feel gorgeous and happy while following you around on your wedding day is probably better.

Contracts

Hiring wedding vendors isn't just about finding someone you personally mesh with; it's also about signing a legally binding contract. Though oral contracts can often be enforced when there is a problem, that is a headache you don't need. So get it in writing. Make sure you have a contract with all of your wedding vendors, even if (perhaps especially if) they are a friend of a friend. Just because you get along with the person you hired doesn't mean you shouldn't both be protected in case something goes awry. Your contract should stipulate the deposit needed to secure your date and when your remaining payments should be made. It should lay out what happens if one of you is unable to fulfill the contract, and it should offer you protections if the contract is not fulfilled up to the standards stated. Perhaps most important, you should feel comfortable negotiating respectfully with your vendors if their standard contract has a clause that makes you uncomfortable. Contracts are a starting point for discussion, not the ending point. Anything that makes you uneasy should be discussed before you sign the contract.

Your Wedding Party: The Bridal Brigade and Beyond

For many of us, a major wedding planning decision is figuring out what our wedding party should look like. On the surface, it seems like picking bridesmaids and groomsmen should be easy, but in reality it's often not. First, and most fundamentally, the wedding party is a way to honor important people in your lives. These people should reflect your life as it's lived, not an attempt to style your life so that it looks like a magazine picture.

The Fundamentals

- You don't need the exact same number of attendants as your partner.

- Attendants do not need to be split along gender lines (your best guy friend can and should stand up for you).

- Your attendants do not have to wear matching outfits.

- You do not have to give your attendants expensive gifts. If you want to give them something, give them a framed picture of you both on your wedding day, and a heartfelt letter. Friendship is free, and don't let anyone convince you otherwise.

The Somewhat More Advanced Concepts

- You don't have to have your attendants stand up for you, and instead can find other ways to honor them (readings, songs, symbolic religious duties).

- You don't have to have formal attendants (we had a ragtag bunch of old and new friends, whom we called our bridal brigade and who pitched in to help at our wedding).

- You don't have to have attendants at all.

The Really Advanced Concepts

For most of us, the wedding party isn't completely painless. The reality is, many of us don't have tons of people willing to drop all their plans and fly across the country to throw us bridal showers, or five size-two friends who look good in eggshell blue, or four girls we've been best friends with since we were five. Maybe we don't even *have* piles of best friends. And that's fine. The point is to

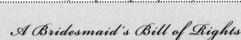

A Bridesmaid's Bill of Rights

When you ask someone to be your bridesmaid, it's easy to start thinking that normal rules don't apply. You're getting married, after all, and chances are, you're extremely excited about this huge party being thrown in your honor. You can get sucked into thinking that the wedding is as important to everyone else as it is to you and throw common sense out the window. But before you do, some thoughts:

- People in your life are not going to change their fundamental personalities just because they are your bridesmaids. If your best friend is a disorganized mess, expect that to continue when she's your maid of honor.

- Keep your wedding party's real-life budget in mind. If you're asking your ladies to wear expensive dresses, consider offering to pay for them.

- Think about overall cost. Your wedding party isn't just paying for their outfits, they are also paying for their travel, your gifts, and maybe bridal shower or bachelorette party expenses as well. Be thoughtful with what you ask from them financially, and remember to show your gratitude.

- Showers and bachelorette parties are optional. If someone offers to throw you a shower, thank them. If you throw yourself a

[continues]

find a way to honor people we love and to have people around us on our wedding day who make us feel supported. Maybe you want a traditional wedding party in all matching dresses. Maybe you just want a group of women who love you and support you and take your phone calls when you're freaking out about your wedding. Just know that there is no one way to do things and that wedding parties are always a little imperfect, just like friendships.

bachelorette party, remember the time and energy people are putting into coming, and thank them again. Most important, if some of your wedding party can't attend these events, be understanding. (I swear, they still love you!)

- Ask their opinions. Wedding Land is not always the most rational place to be. So if you're convinced that the lime-green fluffy ball gowns are the best bridesmaid dresses ever, and your ladies are . . . less convinced . . . listen to them. If they try to talk you off a stress ledge, keep listening.

- Remember the purpose of your wedding party. They are there to hold your hand when you're stressed, support you on your wedding day, and stand up for you and your marriage for the rest of your life. The dresses they wear are pretty but are really just the tiniest of details.

A note to bridesmaids: Remember, your job is to make the bride's life easier (while still being your charming self). Getting married is stressful in ways that are sometimes hard to comprehend from the outside. So ask the bride how she's feeling and what you can do to support her. And if she still insists that the lime-green fluffy ball gown is stunning, suck it up, and celebrate your ass off in that sucker. She's going to owe you a lot of drinks when she comes to her senses.

Parties and Showers and Bachelorettes, Oh My

As the modern wedding industry has expanded (and expanded and expanded), more and more parties have made the list of Things You Must Have to Get Married. The current list of tangential-to-the-wedding parties include the engagement party, the wedding shower (or showers), the bachelor party, and the bachelorette party. That is a whole lot of extra parties to worry about when you're dealing with planning one of the biggest celebrations of your life.

Should some of these parties happen to you, you should embrace them and enjoy them. But please don't think that these bashes are (a) traditional and mandatory, (b) something your bridesmaids are required to throw for you, or (c) show how much the people around you love you. In fact, these are optional celebrations you should enjoy if they happen and not worry about if they don't. And no, you can't require people to throw them for you (though you can nicely ask for help, or even throw the parties for yourself, if they really matter to you).

Wedding Style: What Matters, What Doesn't

When planning a wedding, decisions about how things are going to look tend to take up a lot of brain space. Wedding media tend to focus on the pretty bits, and it's fun to get absorbed with planning the little details. What kind of table numbers are you going to have? What style of wedding dress do you want? What is your color palette? Weddings are pretty. Pretty is fun. And the pretty stuff can be a good way to distract you from the harder parts of the process. So if the details are enjoyable to you, by all means, embrace this part of wedding planning.

But if at any point the pretty parts of wedding planning stop being fun and start making you crazy, take a deep breath and reassess. Michelle Edgemont, who married in a public

The Dress (From Sparkles to Meringue and Back)

The dress. If there are two more weighty words in wedding planning, I'm not sure what they are. Somehow the modern wedding industry has managed to convince us that all of our marital hopes and dreams are wrapped up in this one piece of (pretty, pretty) clothing. That would be great, if wedding dresses were not so expensive and homogeneous. If you're having a hard time finding a dress that you can afford and that fits your style, here are some tried and true options.

- *Buy a white bridesmaid's dress.* If you're looking for a relatively simple dress but you want a wedding-y style, look into buying a bridesmaid's dress in white or ivory. You can even splurge and get a big-name designer's dress for a fraction of what their wedding dresses cost. This is a great way to get lovely, lacy, frothy confections for a much lower price. Plus, chances are you'll be able to pee alone.

- *Buy a vintage dress.* This option involves more than a little luck and often requires that you fit easily into vintage sizes. But when it works, it works. I got my 1950s wedding dress for $250 on San Francisco's Haight Street, and it was beautiful: tea length, with pleated tulle and lace. You can look at online vintage wedding-dress boutiques (usually the more expensive option, because they specialize in the bridal market), or at vintage stores in any urban area.

- *Hack your dress.* Buy a simple, affordable wedding dress from a place like Target, J Crew, or Craigslist. You can hire a seamstress to add bells and whistles, or you can hack into it yourself. I've seen women add complicated appliqué, cut asymmetrical hemlines, add ruffles, sew swatches of lace all over the skirt, add hand-sewn flowers, or just add a sash. And the best part? If you buy a dress that's less than $100 and screw it up? You can probably afford to start over.

- *Make a dress.* If you or a loved one can sew, what on earth are you waiting for? This option allows you complete control over style and materials.

[continues]

- *Buy a prom dress or a* quinceañera *dress.* If you're not too fussy about high-quality materials and just want a pretty dress, look into these dresses. You get all the ruffles and glamour of a wedding dress (in white or in a bright color, your choice), all at a teenager's price point.

- *Buy a regular white dress.* So you found a white cotton summer dress that you love? Who says it's not wedding-y enough? Trust me, on your wedding day you will look like a bride.

- *Buy a used dress.* There are lots of websites specializing in selling preworn wedding dresses. This makes a massive amount of sense, given that these dresses were worn exactly once (if that—lots of oops-I-got-a-second-dress dresses end up on these sites), and they are generally 25 percent to 50 percent off.

- *Buy a discount dress.* Discount wedding dress stores get a bad rap, but there is something to be said for dresses that look exactly like the big-name designer dresses at a fraction of the cost. If you go to these stores, never give them your contact information, as they will spam you into the ground. But do bring a passel of girlfriends and expect to have some fun. And hey, if you walk out with a knock-off dress that you love? Be proud.

- *Buy a regular wedding dress and rock the hell out of it.* Maybe all of these options sound too complicated for you, and your mom really wants to buy you a full-price wedding dress (or you want to buy it for yourself). If you're tempted by that idea, go for it. There is not a single reason in the world why you can't take a lovely, lacy, silky wedding dress and own it.

- *Don't wear a dress at all.* Maybe you hate dresses or maybe you just hate white. Then you shouldn't wear a dress and you shouldn't wear white. On your wedding day you should feel like your most true self. And if that means wearing a pantsuit or a bright orange cocktail dress? You should do it.

social hall in Pennsylvania, went through some serious wedding planning stress before she had a revelation: "I unsubscribed from any blog that made me feel inferior, crazy, self-conscious, or dumb. This is an important piece of advice to all engaged ladies: those feelings are not what wedding planning is about. If you have them, go right now and take a good, hard look at all wedding media you are digesting and make a strong choice to not be a part of anything that makes you feel bad." When planning your wedding aesthetics stops being a fun project and starts being a maddening quest to keep up, it's time to take a step back.

The Details: How They Matter, How They Don't

Back in Chapter 1, I made you tack up the phrase "I will not remember how my wedding looked, I will remember how my wedding felt," in a place where you could see it every day. Though you should be thinking about that with every decision you make, you still probably need to make decisions about your wedding aesthetics. Nicole Kazee, who had a pig roast at her reception in a small resort town in Michigan, said, "You're going to have to make a million little decisions, regardless of whether you actually care or not, but the focus should be on choosing big things that will shape the spirit of it all—things that get you wildly, deeply excited." For example, before Anna Shapiro's interfaith wedding, she had people craft quilt squares to sew into the chuppah they married under. In this way, the aesthetics became important because they allowed people to be included in the ritual of marriage. She said, "I was sure that on the actual day I would feel like an idiot for having put so much energy into unimportant details. But when I looked around this room full of most of the people that I love in this world, all having an awesome time, I was overwhelmed with the feeling that we had created this. I don't regret spending time on the details, not because of the aesthetics, but because they all came together to make us all feel loved, special, included, excited, and all manner of other cool things."

The wedding industry tells you that the details matter because your crafty place cards will make your wedding stand out. And that's not really true. Your place cards won't make your wedding yours, but your love will. That's not to say that the details won't matter. They will, but not in the way you expect. As people, we experience life as a collection of moments and details. When you look back at your wedding, it will be a collection of little things that stand out. It might be the rich chocolate cake you covered in dahlias, or the way your tea-length dress swirled when you danced. These are the kind of details you'll remember, and they are also the things you can never truly plan. So focus your energy on the things that get you excited. Think of them as markers on the trail, pointing you toward your wedding joy.

What Matters Most: Key Wedding Elements

Some elements of your wedding are more impactful than others. Even if you are in love with your bridesmaids' dresses, your venue is going to affect the way people perceive your wedding a whole lot more. Often these high-impact facets of wedding planning don't get a lot of airplay in wedding media because they don't photograph well, or aren't expensive, or are not easy to talk about in print. But if you want to throw a lazy and chic wedding, these are the things you should focus on:

- Location: About 33 percent of your pictures will be dominated by your location. (Please note the precision with which I made this calculation.) No matter how hard you try, it's impossible to make a wedding inside a hotel ballroom look like it took place in an English garden on a warm summer day. You will save yourself a whole lot of heartache if you stop trying to force the issue and just pick a location you like.

- The people: For those of you following my math at home, the happy faces of the people you love will dominate the other 66 percent of your pictures. Which is to say, when you leave a great party, you're normally raving about how fantastic the people were, not about how the favors perfectly matched the tablecloths. So, if you focus on inviting people you love, chances are good you're going to have a pretty awesome party.

- The officiant: Have you ever been to a wedding where the officiant makes awful jokes, seems to have never met the couple in question, and robotically conducts a service that should be emotional? Yeah. You're going to want to avoid that. We'll talk more about finding the right officiant in Chapter 8, but until then, mark this choice down as "reasonably important."

- The food: The type of food you serve sets the tone for the kind of party you want to have (and expensive food does not necessarily mean a better vibe). A sit-down, steak dinner signals one thing to guests; a jazz brunch buffet reception signals something else. Think about your food choices, and make sure they line up with the kind of party you want to throw.

- The dress: Though there is way too much focus on having the perfect wedding dress, one of the most obvious signals you can give your guests about the type of party you're having is the dress you're wearing. A slinky, 1920s-style shift gives off a totally different vibe than a huge, frothy, strapless ball gown. You shouldn't spend a fortune on your dress, but you might want to fight to wear a dress you like a lot.

- The photography: Here is a dirty little secret: a good photographer (and I don't necessarily mean an expensive photographer) can make any wedding look stylish. A bad photographer can make the world's most expensive and chic wedding look like a hot mess. If you want to remember your wedding day as tremendously hip, hire your photographer carefully, and stop stressing about the little details.

- Everything else: Once you've focused on getting a few key elements right, you're close to home free. Beyond that, focus only on what seems fun to you. Maybe you are looking forward to choosing the flowers. Maybe you don't care about how the wedding looks, but you want a throw-down dance party. Figure out what those elements are, and do them well. If you have beautiful flowers but no other decorations, people will remember how tasteful your wedding was. If you attempt twenty-seven craft projects, but all of them are a little bit of a mess, well, that's how it's going to look (and you are going to be a total stress ball).

Once you've figured out what stylish wedding elements you care about, let everything else go. Repeat after me: I do not need all the wedding elements that people tell me I need. I will have a cake if I want a cake; I will have favors if I want favors; I will have flowers if I want flowers. If I do not care about these things I will not have them, and I will not feel guilty. And most of my guests will not even notice.

That Color-Coded Spreadsheet Is Actually Worth It

The ability for you—and those around you—to be laid-back on your wedding day depends heavily on well-laid plans. As someone who used to plan events for a living, let me tell you, the most relaxed events feel that way because the event planner busted her ass making plans and then making contingency plans. In my family, the story is that at the end of their wedding day, my mom said to my dad, "All those months of planning, and it felt like it went by so fast." And my dad rather pragmatically responded, "If you hadn't done all that planning, today would have felt like it dragged on forever." And *that* is not the kind of forever you're looking for on your wedding day.

Events with a large number of people (and by large I mean more than four) and multiple vendors (by which I mean more than just the officiant) need to be planned. That's the bottom line. The tricky part is that for most couples, this is the first major event they've ever had to plan. Hello, deep end! This is you being thrown in. But never fear. The basic guidelines for planning an event are straightforward, and we are going to walk through them together. Marchelle Farrell summed it up best when she told me, "Let us be clear: unless you are an event manager or lead a life quite wonderfully different to mine, your wedding is likely to be the first big event you organize and host. But when you get down to the nitty-gritty of it, planning a wedding is essentially taking a series of decisions and making sure certain tasks get done." And that you can do.

Some people would read all this and tell you, "And that's why you need a wedding planner." But you don't. Not really. You might want a wedding planner. If you can afford a wedding planner, you might even decide it's worth it to you. But at the end of the day, you don't *need* a wedding planner. Did your grandmother have a wedding planner? I rest my case. What you do need is some system of organization that works for you, and a wedding stage manager (see Chapter 9) to hand everything over to the day before your wedding.

The first part of getting organized is figuring out what sort of system is going to make sense for you. Some people work best with Post-it notes and piles of paper. Other people like wedding binders—everything in hard copy, with lots of room to paste in pictures clipped from magazines for inspiration. Some couples fall in love with online all-in-one planners—web-based products you can even use from your phone. Me, I'm an old-school event-planner type. I like a good spreadsheet. Spreadsheets give you one central place where you can enter and sort information, and share it with whoever needs it.

Wedding Planning Spreadsheets

Here is a list of some of the spreadsheets you might find useful to create for wedding planning. Do not let this list overwhelm you. Remember, this is supposed to make your life easier, not more complicated. And don't worry, on your wedding day, you won't be in charge of any of these.

- Guest list and RSVP: It's helpful to include guest addresses here, too.

- Tasks that must get done and the person in charge of the task: This will also help you and your partner in the early stages of planning.

- Vendor contacts: You may end up talking to more than a few vendors, and if you keep their contact information and details organized, it will be easier for both you and your partner.

- Important information for your wedding week: This should include flight information, hotel information, etc.

- A wedding-weekend spreadsheet: What are the events? What needs to happen to make each event successful? Who is in charge of these tasks?

- Hauling spreadsheet: What needs to get delivered to your wedding site, who is going to get it there, and when?

- The all-important day-of spreadsheet: This is perhaps the most key document in wedding planning. It outlines every activity that will take place on your wedding day, with a time, location, and a person selected to be in charge (see Chapter 9).

Trust Yourself

And finally, trust yourself. This might be the hardest wedding planning advice to follow, but it's probably the most important. When you're planning your wedding, you'll have a lot of outside input clamoring for your attention. It's easy to start to think that there is some sort of wedding standard you need to live up to, or a particular aesthetic that's best for your wedding. This isn't true.

What is important is that you pick elements for your wedding that you like. If you're debating whether this thing goes with this other thing, just remember, if you like all the items you picked for your wedding, then they've got one thing in common: they'll make you grin on your wedding day. Pick stuff that makes you happy, and then stop obsessing. Seriously. Stop it.

And use that time you gained to do something worthwhile—practice for married life. Kristiina Hackel, who married for the second time in a historic home in Southern California, put it this way: "I know that a marriage, like every relationship, needs to be protected, invested in, and prioritized. You probably know this too, but let me add that the wedding is a good place to practice this. After all, you are not marrying your florist (although it may feel that way at times). Yes, the photo booth needs attention—but maybe you should just go out and see a movie instead." Got that? Now take a deep breath, step away, and go hang out with your partner. After all, this person is the reason you're in this delightful pickle in the first place.

THE PRACTICAL BRIDE REMEMBERS . . .

- Wedding planning is not going to change your fundamental nature. So focus on what you're good at, and forget (or hire people to help with) the rest.

- When making wedding decisions, remember that the best is the enemy of the good. Lots of good-enough decisions can make something pretty great, so just make the decision already.

- Hire vendors you like and trust. You'll work closely with them, and it's not worth sacrificing sanity for style.

- Your wedding party is a way to honor important people in your life. So forget whatever you think the rules are, and focus on what works for you and your loved ones.

- Engagement parties, showers, and bachelorette parties are strictly optional.

- When planning your wedding style, focus most of your energy on the big, high-impact decisions, and less on the details.

- Come up with a system for organizing your wedding planning information early in the process. I suggest spreadsheets.

- Trust yourself. Choose things that will make you grin on your wedding day.

6

DOING IT YOURSELF
(TOGETHER)

DIY: Brilliant and Crazy

Over the past few years, do-it-yourself (DIY) has snuck to the forefront of the wedding landscape. Suddenly it seems that everyone is making it from scratch, whether "it" consists of hand-painted wedding invitations or the dress. And handmade is suddenly such big business that a whole industry is dedicated to helping you spend money to make "it" your own. It's as if our options have been narrowed down to mind-bogglingly expensive and big budget, or lovingly handcrafted in an indie-chic way, with relatively little middle ground.

I remember the first time I read about a DIY wedding project. I was twenty-two and single, and I'd sneakily bought a copy of a wedding magazine to read on the subway (I was *that girl* sometimes, and I have no shame about it). The article detailed how to make baskets for your flower girls. I remember thinking, "Planning a wedding is stressful enough! Why on earth would you want to make these stupid baskets that you could clearly buy at a ninety-nine-cent store?" Fast-forward seven years, and I was pouring cement for our DIY chuppah. Of course.

My twenty-two-year-old self was more than a little bit right: DIYing a million projects for your wedding can be a huge pain in the ass and a demanding addition to an already stressful event. But my twenty-nine-year-old self was also on to something: DIYing elements of your wedding can be rewarding, if undertaken in moderation. In this chapter we'll talk about sensible ways to tackle DIY: understanding why you're taking on a task, and picking projects that won't make you crazy. Plus, we'll delve into some DIY projects that might actually be worth it in the final cost-benefit analysis. But through it all, remember, although DIY is often just what's necessary to throw a wedding you can afford and is sometimes a fabulous distraction from the stress, it's not the point. DIYing is one facet of how you're celebrating a really big deal: the future you're building together.

Why DIY? Knowing Your Goal

There are many reasons to make things for your wedding. Some are good, and some are . . . slightly less good. The trick is to figure out why you want to make things, and then decide whether making things is actually a good idea.

DIY to Save Money

There is a whole contingent of you who are staring at the book right now, pondering throwing it across the room. You just yelled, "Why am I DIYing, you idiot? Because I have no money, so I have to!" And, point. Liz Moorhead put it this way: "Our wedding was crafty and DIY, not because we're cool indie kids. Because we're broke." Modern wedding media often make DIY sound like a trend, but for many of us it's just the reality of having a wedding. Even so, if approached sanely, DIY can lead to meaningful experiences that you might not have had with a more expensive wedding. As Liz said, "Some of, maybe all of, my favorite parts of the wedding were the result of cut corners to fit the budget." The time you spend with loved ones making your wedding happen matters and gets you ready for the day itself.

When DIYing to keep on budget, be selective about what projects you take on. No matter what you think going in, DIY does not always save you money. If you're undertaking a complicated craft that you know very little about, you might end up spending more money on supplies as you flounder around learning what you're doing, than you would just hiring someone to do it for you. Before you start a project, ask yourself the following questions:

- Is this item a must-have at our wedding?

- Can we afford to hire someone to help us with it?

- If not, is it simple enough for us to take on and still stay within our budget?

DIY to Keep Your Hands Busy

One of the most time-honored reasons to make things for your wedding is to keep your hands busy and your mind calm. When contemplating a life change, it's helpful to keep your brain focused on what you can control. Britta Nielsen, who

DIY Wedding (It Wasn't About the Details)

BY CARA FORBES-STENNING

What did I learn from getting married? Many things: if you're doing it yourself, ask for help—loads of it; you don't need as many boxes of biscuits as you have guests; spending your monthly food budget on fancy cheese is unnecessary; and if you take medication that alters your mood, taking it upon yourself to lower the dose a fortnight before your wedding is a bad idea. But which of these things to expand on, which might offer some insight to other brides-to-be? I'll go for the one that I wish I'd realized earlier.

It's not about the details.

Hardly a novel idea, I know. Wise women have been telling us this since the very beginning, but love-struck fools like me (I'm assuming I'm not the only one) have been ignoring it.

I love the details. The details were my sustenance during the bitter moments of wedding planning. Handmaking prettinesses made me smile (and occasionally want to throw things out the window, but that's par for the course, right?), and I firmly believed they would make our wedding . . . better, somehow.

Well, they didn't. It wasn't the details we managed to pull off that made me realize this; it was the huge number of projects that didn't quite make it to the wedding day, either because we just didn't have time to finish them or because on the morning of the wedding we were too busy making sure our guests would have tables to eat at to worry about fripperies like decor. The aisle decorations never made it, but even better than admiring our beautiful silk ribbons, our guests admired the love and joy that shone out of our ceremony. Escort cards? Well, I spent days making them, but again, and I know not how or why, we ended up with a list of names written on a piece of card, and no lives were lost as people found their seats without the help of handwritten notes hung on a washing line with bird-shaped pegs.

Finally, the one thing that really brought it home to me that the details matter less than the thought behind them: the photo line. We fantasized about a string of photos hung outside and fluttering in the breeze. Photos of us at every stage in our lives, with our family members and friends, hung where all could admire them. We spent hours choosing just the right photos and a fortune having them printed. We bought ribbon that coordinated

[continues]

with the rest, two bamboo sticks to string them between, and a hundred wooden clothes-pegs to hang them up with. On the morning of the wedding we got as far as putting the sticks in the ground before we were confronted with a worrying lack of dinner tables and ceremony chairs, and the photos were abandoned in a sorry pile at the bottom of a cardboard box and swiftly forgotten about. Until much later in the day, that is, when a bridesmaid found them slightly squashed and in a terribly unattractive yellow cardboard packet. She took them out, divvied them up into three piles, and handed them round. People held a half-eaten cupcake in one hand and a handful of photos in the other as they congregated in groups to laugh, reminisce, cringe, and get tearful. The photos were a huge hit with everyone.

People who had never met before shared giggles at my mum dressed (very convincingly) as a Mexican man; friends saw pictures of parties they had hosted and remembered what it was like back in the old days; and girlfriends saw their boyfriends as little fat, naked babies and cooed delightedly. Nobody would have enjoyed them more if they had been hanging beautifully in a line. Nobody cared that the yellow packet didn't match the invitations or that the photos weren't in chronological order. What they did care about was that they were given a chance to come together, to tell new friends old tales, to remember other occasions where we had all been together.

The details can be pretty. They can give your guests something to admire, remember, and talk about. Spend time on them if you want to; spend time on them if you enjoy it. But know this one thing: your guests care about the thought, not the execution. The things your guests really want to admire, talk about, and remember? The love they share for you and each other. Think about the memories you will make, not the photos that your details will make. I won't deny that the compliments I got on the little things made me smile—"Oh, you like the matchboxes? Why thank you; they took me hours to make"—but the self-satisfied glow that I get from remembering those moments is as insignificant as a sparkler to the sun when I think about the sight of our friends and families coming together and talking and laughing, really laughing, about the history and the future we were building and celebrating. That is what matters; those are the memories that will fill you with love once it is over. Not the escort cards, not the aisle decorations, and not the cursed invitations.

works as an industrial designer, told me, "As wedding planning continued, it turned out I'd rather have my hands busy as an anti-anxiety measure. I made a lot of wedding stuff. To anyone confused about why people get all crafty around wedding time: it kept me sane. And it was fun." Making wedding crafts because it's relaxing is an excellent plan. But the minute you feel it making you insane? Put down what you're working on and step back.

DIY Because You Like to Make Things (Hooray!)

Here is what I'd figured out by the time I was twenty-nine years old and helping to pour the cement for our chuppah: I like to make things. I really like to make things with my husband. For our wedding, I had an overwhelming need to create things that reflected who we were, not how we shopped. So while we built our chuppah to reflect our taste, the real point was that it was ours. We'd made it with our own two hands. It didn't make our wedding better, but it let us feel more ownership of it. Plus, we enjoyed spending time together making the chuppah. This is possibly the best reason to DIY for your wedding: you enjoy it.

DIY to Create Indie-Chic Perfection (Uh-Oh)

So money isn't your primary concern, you don't feel the need to keep your hands busy, and in fact, you don't really like making stuff by hand. It's possible, in your heart of hearts, that you're considering crafting projects for your wedding because it will make your wedding somehow, um, better. The wedding media is full of weddings where everything was made by hand and gorgeous. Of course, a little digging will reveal that "made by hand" often means "made by a team of professionals to look like it was made by hand." There is nothing wrong with this, but if you don't have a team of professionals, it's really important to understand what crafts made by amateurs actually look like. (Hint: nothing like the crafts you see in wedding magazines.)

Drill into your head the phrase coined by Anna Shapiro while planning her wedding: "Aesthetics are not ethics." It's fine to have a bunch of handcrafted projects if you like making things. But having a wedding that looks handcrafted does not mean it is more authentic, grounded, or somehow better. DIY because you need to; DIY to keep your hands busy; DIY because it's fun. But don't DIY because it's better. It's not better. It's just more time consuming.

DIT: Do-It-Together

As modern weddings have become increasingly focused on the individuality of the couple getting married, they have become ever more isolating to plan. As a culture, we've moved from weddings creating an opportunity for a community to come together and celebrate, to forcing major event planning on a couple, or a bride, undergoing a significant life transition. To bring some sanity and some joy back into wedding planning, I suggest that we shift our focus from do-it-yourself (DIY) to do-it-together (DIT). It's tempting to think that you have to create everything for your wedding on your own. The wedding media emphasizes the idea that weddings are a time to embrace personalization—to create something that perfectly reflects every aspect of who you are. But weddings are more than that. They are a reflection of you, of your community, and of the people who love you. So consider asking and allowing your loved ones to help you DIY. To do it together.

Shana Pellitteri, who threw an interfaith, family-centric, laughter-filled wedding at her husband's family home in the Catskills, told me, "The wedding process taught me a lot of things, and one of the best was how to play to people's strengths. Know what they're good at, find out what they enjoy doing, and ask them to do it. If you're coming from the right place, they'll say yes." After you've asked for help, remember to surrender some creative control. Flowers arranged by the women in your family are not going to look the same way as flowers arranged by you, alone in a room. But by relinquishing some control, you replace flowers that reflect your exacting personal taste with flowers that represent other people's love for you (and besides, you can always exert a little bit of secret quality control later).

DIT-ish (Get Some Help)

DIT doesn't have to be something you do together with your families. It can also be something you do by enlisting a little help from professionals and combining it with your own (slightly lazy) desire to be crafty. In today's hipster DIY culture, it's easy to think that the only way to handcraft invitations is to go whole hog—make your own paper from recycled newspaper, carve wooden block stamps that you hand ink, and decorate the envelope with calligraphy that you taught yourself. But of course this is nonsense. You can design an invitation and send it to an online mass printer. You can buy predesigned invitation files and use the image to print your invitations by hand. You can mix professional help with handcrafting, and get help from people you pay instead of people you love.

DIT with Your Loved Ones

If you really want your loved ones to help but are not sure how to make that happen, remember: you don't need a collection of graphic designers, seamstresses, and photographers at your beck and call. You just need willing bodies. If people seem stressed when you ask them to help with your wedding, explain to them that you are just looking for help, not for substitute professionals. Shana Pellitteri's extended family spent the week before the wedding baking and preparing for the party, and she advises, "If you think this could never happen with your family and friends, neither did we. It could. Create it. A wedding is such a remarkable opening to get people present to raw emotion." Explain to your family that you just want your community to rally around you. You want a little barn raising at your wedding. You're doing things the old-fashioned way—you're doing it together.

But be honest with yourself. Not all families are the type that rally together to throw a wedding by hand, and it's not always worth forcing the issue. There are times when you have to own up to the fact that your family is not crafty or just does not want to do hard work to make your wedding happen. Allow your loved ones to show their support in ways that make sense to them, through labor, through money, or through hugs. DIY won't save the world, and it won't save your wedding. So focus on saving your sanity instead. You are going to need it later.

Practical Ways to DIY

So you've thought about DIY, and the bottom line is—you're going to be taking on some projects for your wedding and you'd like some tips on how to best handle them. In this section we'll discuss some major wedding undertakings: doing your wedding flowers, DJing your wedding, having family and friends contribute to your photography, and self-catering. It's unlikely that you'll want to take on all of these projects at once, unless you have a small wedding, or a lot of people helping you out, or both. But in this era of high wedding prices and expectations, many of us need to take on at least one of these projects.

Here are some tips to help you figure out how to navigate these aspects of your wedding—to help you decide what you can and can't manage yourself. Remember, every project you choose to DIY takes time; don't kid yourself about that. Part of choosing DIY projects wisely is thinking with your time-management hat on. So if you're self-catering, please think twice about making three hundred matchbook covers. You can thank me later.

How to DIY Wedding Flowers

If you're planning to DIY the wedding flowers, first decide whether you want to make your bouquets or your centerpieces, or both. Making bouquets is a simple exercise, and don't let anyone tell you otherwise. There are lots of straightforward tutorials on how to make a round, hand-tied bouquet, and with a little research, you'll do just fine. If, however, you're making bouquets and a selection of flower arrangements, you'll need to devote a bit more energy to planning and logistics.

SOURCES FOR WEDDING FLOWERS

- A wholesale flower market: If you live in or near an urban area and are looking for a large quantity of flowers, consider shopping at your local flower market. Most flower markets have hours for the general public and are a great source for a large variety of affordable in-season flowers.

- Online flower wholesalers: There are increasing numbers of reputable online flower sellers who will ship fresh flowers for you to arrange. Talk to their customer service departments to figure out when the flowers should be delivered and whether the blooms will need time to open.

- Your local grocery store: If you're just looking to make bouquets, you can absolutely visit your local grocery store, gourmet food store, or big-box store the day before the wedding and buy whatever they have on hand for your bouquets. It's a quick, affordable, and super low-stress solution.

WEDDING FLOWER TIPS

- Do a dry run. Testing things out and playing around will make you much more confident and speedy the weekend of your wedding.

- Order your supplies in advance. My suggestions: floral tape, floral scissors, pins, floral foam, vases.

- Do your flowers the day before. It's tempting to try to schedule doing your flowers on the morning of your wedding. Unless you are doing the simplest of arrangements, resist the urge to over-schedule.

- You need helpers. Putting together flowers is fun, but a lot of construction work. Pick a team of people who will be calm, focused, and enjoy putting together pretty things.

- Set up a sample or two, and let people copy that. Your helpers may not know as much about flowers as you (now) do, and they are going to obsess about getting it right.

- Set up quality control. If you have a lot of hands working and you're attached to the output, have someone with a trusted eye tweaking the end product.

- You don't need the world's biggest bouquet. Handmade bouquets are often overly large because hey, they can be. Keep in mind you want your bouquet to be on scale with your body, so go smaller than you think you need.

- Make boutonnieres and corsages the day of (or skip them). These pieces are delicate and tend to die if made in advance.

- Stop worrying about refrigeration. You're not going to be able to refrigerate everything overnight. Put your arrangements in a cool, shady place and stick your bouquets in water in a fridge. That will be good enough.

- If you are transporting your arrangements, consider using floral foam. It will make the arrangements snug, in case they fall over in transport. If you are using floral foam, you'll want to use opaque vases.

- Make sure you have enough transportation if you can't make the arrangements on-site. Flowers take up quite a bit of space, and you will need several cars with trunk space or a large van.

- Realize that doing your own flowers isn't cheap; it's just cheaper. Flower costs, along with supplies and vases, tend to add up. If you want an even more affordable solution, consider skipping centerpieces and just make simple bouquets.

How to DJ Your Wedding

There are a lot of horror stories circulating about self-DJed weddings. You may have been told that if you DIY the wedding music, there will be no party energy, and everything will fall apart. None of this has to be true if you do some advance planning.

- Amplification matters. What makes the difference between a successful DIY dance party and one that falls flat is amplification. For people to lose themselves in the music, it needs to be loud. Look into renting an affordable professional amplification system that you can run with a computer.

- Cross-fade. Set up your playlist to cross-fade (and to cut endless songs down to size). Dance parties don't like dead air.

- Play music people know. You may have obscure taste in music, but if you load up your playlist with tons of songs people don't know, you will end up with a rousing bar scene instead of a packed dance floor. You want people to say, "I love this song!" over and over again, as they run for the dance floor.

- Play a mix of music for all ages. Yeah, you might like Lauryn Hill, but I'm pretty sure your granny likes Billie Holiday singing the standards, so mix it up.

- Think about the flow of your playlist. For a successful dance party, you want to build up the energy, ease it down so people can rest and slow dance, and then build it up even higher. Continue this pattern till you build up the energy to a near frenzy at the end, and then end with a sweet, slow, and emotional last dance.

- Have a music bouncer. The quickest way to kill a dance party is to have guests adjusting the music midstream. So pick a music bouncer, and make sure that person is tough.

- Don't be afraid to adjust your own playlist. Though your guests can't touch the playlist, you and your music bouncer absolutely can. Load up your iPod with more music than you need, and if you get to a point where the music doesn't match the mood, just skip ahead on your playlist.

- Don't be afraid to pick a few emotional and obscure favorites. We ended our wedding with an obscure medley by Sam Cooke. That was when I finally let go, tears streaming down my cheeks. Our friends might not have known the song before our wedding, but they sang with all their hearts in those last moments as they formed a circle around us, a moment I'll remember forever.

- You'll have the playlist for the rest of your life. Enough said.

How to DIY the Wedding Photography

It's easy to fall into the trap of putting way too much emphasis on chic wedding pictures. Though a great wedding photographer can be a worthwhile investment (and is the single easiest way to make your wedding look stylish in retrospect), it's not necessary. Think of wedding albums from our parents' generation. There are generally only a handful of pictures, but they still allow you to appreciate the moment. In the end, we frame a few wedding pictures, and we put the rest in an album. Our lives move on, and the album goes on the shelf where it will one day get pulled down by a tiny daughter, or niece, or granddaughter who will peer at the dusty pages admiringly. It won't matter to her how much you spent on those pictures, just how happy you were, and how pretty you looked (and you're always going to look pretty to your tiny niece).

If you can't afford a wedding photographer (or don't care to have one), here are some tips for collecting pictures from friends and loved ones:

- Explicitly ask people to help in advance. It's not a nice surprise to show up at a wedding and find out the couple are expecting you to play wedding photographer just because you have a nice camera. Ask well before the wedding whether friends and loved ones will help, and find a core group of people who are excited to take pictures. Let everyone else know that you'd appreciate it if they'd share whatever pictures they end up taking, but there is no pressure to contribute.

- Set a schedule. If you have lots of people helping out with pictures, create a plan so different people are responsible for different times of the day. Maybe your aunt takes pictures of you getting ready, your girlfriends take pictures of the ceremony, and your teenage cousins shoot the reception. This will ensure most things get photographed, and people still can relax and enjoy the party.

- Write a shot list. If there are certain pictures you want to make sure get taken, or if you want to take formal pictures, write out a shot list. Entrust this list to your wedding stage manager (more on that in Chapter 9) or a good friend. She can work with your helpers and your schedule, and you can stop worrying and just get married.

- Consider providing funky cameras. If you want quirky pictures, consider providing film cameras like a Fuji Instax or a Holga. Let your friends pass around these cameras during the wedding and take shots. You'll have stylish and personal photos. We have an album of friends' Polaroids from our wedding, and they are what I would save if I were running out of the house in a fire.

- Set up a site to collect pictures. If you're depending on lots of people to shoot pictures of your wedding, consider setting up a group in a photo-sharing site as a place for people to upload photos. You can provide flyers for guests with information on how and where to upload the photos.

- Get help. If you still want fancy editing, look into hiring a photographer who will do postproduction on your photos. Once you've collected all the photos, hand them over to a pro to edit your shots to chicness.

- Trust that it will work out. Remember that photos shot by people you love always have a slightly different quality than pictures shot by professionals, and enjoy that. Trust your friends to shoot moments that matter, and enjoy the results. Remember, all you really need is one great wedding picture to frame, and a few other pictures to remember how the day unfolded.

Self-Catering: Less Insane than It Sounds

Often the decision to self-cater your wedding is a purely practical one. If you've determined that you can't afford traditional catering, you may decide that doing it yourself is the most logical solution. Don't let anyone tell you that self-catering is impossible—it is absolutely feasible. People have been self-catering their weddings since time immemorial, largely without world-ending incidents, and you'll be able to do the same. But "self-catering" is a terrifying phrase. Let's break this down into the variety of totally reasonable and manageable options you have at your disposal, and go from there.

Self-Catering Lite

Let's start with what I like to call "self-catering lite." This is where you do your own food, but in a less dramatic way than cooking a sit-down meal for a hundred people. You have lots of options before we get to a steak dinner cooked by your mom and served by waiters in penguin outfits who are really your brothers.

- Dessert reception: The cake-and-punch reception may be the most traditional of all wedding receptions. If you want to self-cater a variation of this party, you can go for the all-dessert reception. It's hard to go wrong with dessert: everything can be made in advance; everything looks beautiful in photographs; and, well, who doesn't like to eat sweets?

- Cocktail party: This party is made up of two key ingredients: cocktails (which are hardly a complicated DIY project) and appetizers. The beauty of appetizers is that you can plan a variety of foods that can be prepared in advance, travel easily, and don't need to be reheated. Plus, you get the fun of a party where everyone is mixing and mingling, not stuck at a table eating.

- Potluck reception: There is no catering option that has more hair-pulling etiquette debate surrounding it than the potluck. But if you have a community of people who are comfortable with potluck parties and live nearby (asking friends who are flying in to bring food is just impractical), and you are impeccable about food safety, this can be a fantastic way to self-cater a wedding. Make sure you provide organization and structure so people know what to bring, and have helpers to sort and serve the food on arrival. Just remember that part (or all) of your guests' gift to you will be the food. That said, if the people you know have never done a potluck in their lives, you might not want to start with your wedding.

Self-Catering, the Whole Hog (So to Speak)

Perhaps self-catering lite is not for you because you are powerful and strong, and you want to tackle the beast. Food for all! Dinner! Let's do it!

Cooking for Large Groups Needs to Be Something You Enjoy

Before we get started, the basics. Do you throw dinner parties? Do you know how to cook? If the answer to these questions is not yes, *please step away.* Your wedding is not the time to take on a massive project that makes you feel like gouging your eyes out, or the time to learn a brand-new skill.

Beyond that, is cooking food something that makes you happy? If you know how to cook for large groups but it makes you feel like sobbing just to think about it, may I suggest a happier project for your wedding? That said, for many families, cooking is the ultimate expression of love. Marie-Ève Laforte self-catered her cocktail reception and told me, "The day before, my mom and I spent the whole day preparing everything. This was a big part of the experience for me, this bonding together in the kitchen, chatting, feeling the buildup of excitement. If anything, it reduced my stress and gave me a great feeling of accomplishment." If the same is true for you, self-catering could be an excellent project to take on.

You Need Help

Do you have help? Seriously. I'm going to ask again: Do you have help? Because you're not going to be self-catering your wedding yourself, nuh-uh, no way. You need people you trust to help you out. You need people who know a thing or two about cooking and who love you enough to put up with plans gone awry and piles of dirty dishes. Once you've found these people, trust them. Ask them for what you need, and believe them when they say they will take care of it.

Stay Organized

Surviving self-catering depends on staying organized and communicating your plan to your helpers (see the "Your Day-Of Spreadsheet" section in Chapter 9 for general organizational hints). Liz Moorhead summed up her organizational strategies this way: "List everything that you need to bring to the venue and home from the venue, have blueprints of where things will be on the table, label the serveware with what kind of food goes in what dish, and on and on. Excel is your friend. So are labels and Post-it notes, and copies of your many lists for any awesome helpers." You can't cook the food months in advance, but you can craft a solid plan.

Select Foods That Make Sense

Your wedding is not the time to try out that complex new coq au vin recipe. In fact, your wedding is not the time to try out any new recipe, period. When selecting a self-catered menu, you're looking for foods that are easy to prepare, travel well, and oh yeah, won't kill your guests (mayonnaise in the hot sun? Absolutely no). Britta Nielsen self-catered her two hundred–person outdoor wedding and had sensible rules: "We only served dishes that involved one step . . . either chopping, grilling, or thawing. Brats and corn on the cob were grilled. Green salad, fruit salad, and bean salad were chopped, and Adam's stepmom heroically made three hundred corn muffins she froze ahead of time that we later thawed." At your wedding reception, complicated is not your friend. Resist the urge to show off.

Supplies

You need more supplies than you think. Borrow serving platters from everyone you know (and tape names to the bottom so you know whom they belong to). Borrow knifes, serving spoons, and silverware. Think through the details: Do you need to rent chafing dishes to keep things warm? Do you need cups and stirrers and sugar for coffee? Do you need tablecloths? Make a list of what you'll need, and then make a plan to come up with the goods.

Setup and Teardown

While you might be helping with the setup (though hopefully you've delegated that), you will not be helping with the teardown or doing the dishes at your own wedding. Make sure you have a plan and volunteers who are willing to help out (and will be responsible for following through, once you've been ushered out the door to your honeymoon).

Food Safety Is Your Number-One Priority

Often discussions of self-catered weddings start verging on the philosophical, with people talking about how "sharing food is sharing love, and sharing love is sharing a community." And that's nice. But if sharing food means sharing a dubious fish-and-mayonnaise dish that was carted in a hot car for six hours . . . well . . . I'm pretty sure the communal act of vomiting was not what you were going for. So. If you're going to self-cater, self-cater. But self-cater with safety.

A Labor of Love

Let's be honest. For most of us, DIY is hard work, undertaken by necessity. It involves lifting boxes, poring over spreadsheets, painstakingly crafting playlists, stripping thorns off roses, and cooking for hours and hours. Most of us don't undertake major wedding DIY because we love crafting but because we have a wedding to throw, and this is how we can actually make it happen. So, if you're feeling overwhelmed by DIY, that is a perfectly reasonable reaction. Ask for help (and lots of it). Figure out what your capacity is, and try not to exceed it. Decide when you can let projects go, or hire someone to help you out with them. And then ask for more help.

Finally, a word of warning: DIY wedding guilt has a way of catching up to you no matter what choices you end up making. If you make lots of things for your wedding, you can be swept up in anxiety that your wedding is going to look cheap. If you made some things for your wedding, you may feel like you should have made more. If you hire professionals for most of your wedding tasks, you can get caught up in worrying that your wedding won't be meaningful or personal enough, or that people will judge you for not being really involved in the planning process. Guilt about wedding DIY can hit you no matter which way you turn, but the truth is, wedding DIY doesn't matter much, other than being a means to an end. What *will* matter is saying your vows and celebrating with those nearest and dearest to you. And those are things that you will certainly do together.

In the end, your wedding is not just one day, it's the accumulation of all the moments that went into creating it. Enjoy the time you spend making your wedding happen with people you love. Try to savor the time spent cooking, or playing with flowers, or figuring out how to sew a wedding dress. Weddings are a labor of love, and when we allow the people around us to share that, sometimes we're lucky enough to create something magical (sweaty, tired, and a little bit stressed, but magical).

THE PRACTICAL BRIDE REMEMBERS . . .

- If you're planning to DIY because you somehow think it will make your wedding better, proceed with caution.

- Consider DIY if it helps you save money, will keep your hands busy, or is just flat-out fun for you. (And stop if it starts making you crazy!)

- Shift the focus of your wedding from do-it-yourself (DIY) to do-it-together (DIT). Get help from family and friends, or get a little professional help with your craftiness.

- Remember to let your loved ones help in their own way—through labor, money, or just hugs.

- If you're DIYing your wedding bouquets, stop stressing; it's a simple and fun project. If you're taking on bouquets and centerpieces, spend a bit more time pre-planning the logistics.

- You can DJ your wedding and have a rousing dance party. Don't let anyone tell you differently. Plan the playlist with care, have good amplification, and enlist a music bouncer.

- If you're having family and friends help with your wedding photography, set a schedule and shot list, and provide a central website for everyone to upload photos.

- When self-catering, consider what kind of food you want to serve. Then assemble a team to help, plan logistics, and always, always remember food safety.

- For most of us, DIY and DIT are hard work and are the reality of how weddings have to get thrown. But your wedding is not just the day itself. Your wedding is all the labor, love, and time that went into it.

7

THE HARD STUFF

Fighting and Crying: It's Normal

After a lifetime of books, movies, and commercials, we all have fixed in our heads the idea that wedding planning is a wonderful time when everyone in our lives comes together to bond over something deeply joyful and to celebrate us. The fact that this idea is so firmly fixed in our brains can make it extra difficult when reality hits and we realize it's not exactly what we imagined.

The hardest part about wedding planning is there is almost always a conflict between what we hoped would be and what is. It's so easy to imagine that your usually emotionally distant mother is going to suddenly warm up and you will pick out

A PRACTICAL BRIDE SPEAKS

Wedding in the Face of Death

BY MORGAN TURIGAN

It was a hard year. In March, my partner, David, learned that he was "temporarily out of work," and my father informed me that he had stage-four lung cancer. Then they discovered cancer in Dad's brain, and he started chemo and radiation. David's return to work was delayed. In July, we decided on a whim to go to Scotland and Ireland. David proposed at a Neolithic portal tomb and it was wonderful. We started to plan a wedding and figured that March, six months away, seemed safe. David went back to work after eight months as my father's health declined. We knew it would be my father's last Christmas, and we tried to paste on smiles. Wedding plans progressed, but it was hard to care.

My father died fifty days before the wedding.

I have very few memories of the week between his death and the wake. I do know that the day after he died, David and I bought a house and were stuck with possession the weekend before the wedding. We packed up, conned friends into helping us move, and ate a lot of takeout. The wedding was wonderful. We went on a lazy beach honeymoon and came home to start setting up house.

A week later, my nineteen-year-old cousin died of a totally unexpected heart problem. He was the spitting image of my father, to the point that at the wake I'd made a joke that as long as we had Michael, it would feel a little bit like young Dad was around. So. Things were hard. The big stuff was very, very hard.

I didn't necessarily cope well. I stopped sleeping. I drank too much rum. I closed the door to my office and cried. The night before my father died, after I left the hospital in the middle of the night, I screamed the entire way home and my voice was left hoarse and raw for a week. I leaned on David—hard—and he caught me when I crumpled. I had anxiety attacks. I made spreadsheets to quell the wedding anxiety. In some ways, having the wedding to focus on was a small blessing—it was a series of tasks that needed to be done, unlike watching my father die in slow motion, where there was nothing to do but watch and grieve.

[continues]

I got grief in waves, and I was fine on the wedding day. The next day? Tired and exhausted and hung over. I made it through the wedding brunch, made it partway home, and then I started to cry. I cried for the next two hours, finally crying myself to sleep in David's arms. My grief came, in part, from managing to get through the wedding without my father, and in part because rites of passage really are a big deal, no matter how happy they make you.

People advised me to move up the wedding date or to involve my father in the planning. That just didn't work for us. Up to the week before he died, my mother was sure he would make it, and I got the feeling that he knew he wouldn't. He lived long enough to meet my husband and to see me happy, and for that I am ever so blessed.

We made sure to celebrate his memory in small ways on the day, and it helped. I wore my father's blue star sapphire engagement ring. The pastor talked about loss and families. My sister's original toast was about my dad, but she wasn't able to handle it and told a funny story about me instead. David's toast to my father made people tear up.

Do I wish my dad was there? Of course. Do I wish he had lived and suffered through a horrible and humiliating illness for two more months just to have watched me wed? Of course not. Do I have any regrets about throwing the wedding, about the timing, about our choices? Sure, everyone has regrets, but I can live with my choices. Do I regret standing up in the room full of family and friends and declaring my love? No, absolutely not. Life is short and it can be cruel; we all know this, so any excuse to celebrate joy should be taken.

Managing to sandwich the wedding in between two funerals makes it abundantly clear to me just how important weddings are. I felt tremendously loved by my family at the wake and the wedding, but the joy at the wedding was healing and wonderful. Talking about grief and death is hard. Celebrating joy in the face of grief is hard, and ever so necessary.

wedding dresses together, giggling and weeping. You imagine that your couldn't-care-less-about-aesthetics fiancé is suddenly going to have opinions about the decor. Maybe you dream that your generally disorganized friend group is going to step up and really pitch in. When one or more of these things don't happen, you can end up a weepy mess, wondering if you're broken.

You're not broken. You're normal.

Wedding planning in America has become a high-stress, high-expense game, and it's more than likely that you're going to encounter some rough patches as you navigate the process. Now, you shouldn't go looking for hard parts. That's borrowing trouble. It is possible that you'll make it through the planning process without weeping once, particularly if you start with realistic expectations and you have a laid-back family. If that happens to you, embrace it. And for goodness' sake, don't worry that you're not doing it right because you're not stressed enough. But if you don't make it through wedding planning scot-free? Know that weddings are often hard and crying is okay.

When I found myself a crying mess during the wedding planning process, I felt guilty. Wasn't I attempting to be a laid-back bride? (And I was, generally, a fairly laid-back bride.) But at the points in the process where I was falling apart, I was falling apart over very real, not-just-wedding-related issues. I was stressed about the realities of merging two families, or painful conflicts with friends, or issues of faith in our new family unit. These were necessary tears, growing-pains tears. Which isn't to discount the tears shed over logistics and money. Those were valid, too.

Wedding planning isn't easy. Perhaps everyone should stop pretending that it is simply an effortless romp through pretty things. In this chapter we'll discuss the fights that come up during wedding planning (they are normal), how to think through cold feet, the myth of the bridezilla (you have good reason to be stressed), and how weddings can be a form of hope when dealing with death or otherwise absent parents. Weddings are like most good things in life: really hard, and really worth it.

Fighting with Your Loved Ones

Chances are good that you're going to have some, uh, difficult moments with your family at some point during the wedding planning process. Even for those of us with generally spectacular, only delightfully crazy families, things go south now and then during this high-stakes, high-emotion time period. As we've discussed, part of the point of the engagement process is learning to set boundaries between your family of origin and your brand-new-baby family. Every disagreement you have over a major issue (like faith) or a seemingly minor issue (like your partner's right to overrule your mom's centerpiece choice) is one step closer to family harmony. You have two long-established families and one brand-new family, and you need to start to figure each other out.

If you're locked in conflict with family members, it can help to try to look at things through their eyes. Ask questions until you figure out what the heck is going on and what they are really upset about. Brianne Sanchez, a journalist who got married on a farm west of Chicago, said, "Here's what it took me a long time to realize: I considered planning our wedding the first endeavor of Joe and mine as new family. My mom considered the wedding the last thing a mother and a daughter do together." This can be the hardest part of wedding planning. You may be outwardly fighting about the dress code for the wedding, but deep down, you might be fighting about what level of formality is appropriate for major life events in your new family, or how hard it is for your parents that you're starting a family of your own. Even if getting married feels like a formality for you, for your mom it might feel a little bit like finally letting go of her baby girl (even if you're forty), and that might be really hard.

Sometimes conflict can be eased by giving parents control over an aspect of the wedding they care about (because who doesn't love a little control?). You can even let your parents do something you would never have chosen on your own, because it matters to them. Cara Winter told me, "Let's face it—your mom has probably been looking forward to this day longer than you have. So if she begs to have welcome bags with an apple theme or to give a guided tour of Brooklyn including places she's never actually been, realize that it's sort of her day, too. And as long as it doesn't betray your values or steal your sanity, it's okay to let others have some control."

Your wedding, like your upcoming family life, is going to be a sometimes-tricky balance. Your job is to draw firm boundaries for things that really matter to your new family and to allow people who love you to participate by doing things they find meaningful. Don't be afraid to fight and cry, and don't be afraid to say no when you really need to. Think of it as practice for the rest of your lives together.

Tension with Your Partner

You and your partner are planning a wedding together, huh? More specifically, you're planning a really large event, with complicated logistics, a big guest list, and issues of faith, values, and money right on the surface. And for the sake of argument, let's just say you've never planned an enormous project together. But it should be easy, right? You should bond, and feel deep joy, and the planning process should bring you closer together than you've ever been. Right? *Right?*

Okay. Reality check. Planning a wedding with your partner is great, in that it's going to teach you how to take on a big endeavor together. You'll probably need these skills later in life for doing things like caring for a sick parent, having kids, renovating a house, or moving across the country. But right now, things might be a little dicey.

The thing is, our partners often think about wedding planning a little differently than we do. My husband certainly did. It's not that he didn't care about the wedding; it's that it tended to be less emotionally loaded for him. During our planning, I learned that my husband didn't have an opinion on everything, much as I wanted him to. Sometimes he didn't want to discuss all possible alternatives, he just wanted to think it through quickly and come to a gut decision (smart man!). Harrison Caudill, an engineer who ended his wedding by flying over it in his favorite airplane, put it this way: "Treat the wedding as you would a project at work. Nothing involved in the process anywhere is a life-and-death decision. If you can't afford something, you find a way around, or you do without."

If you're lucky enough to have a partner who approaches wedding planning differently than you do, embrace it. Start figuring out the differences in how you address problems. Chances are, you picked each other because you make each other better people. Your strategies for planning a wedding just might complement each other as well. At least, after a few fights.

The Bridezilla Myth:
Making You Crazy, then Calling You Crazy

Wedding planning has moved from being something the community (or at least the families) planned for the couple to being an enormous project taken on almost totally in isolation. Add to the fact that, as discussed in Chapter 3, weddings have gotten three to four times as complicated and hugely more expensive in the course of just a few generations. Taking this all together, you have the recipe for disaster.

Unfortunately, none of this is being discussed in polite company—at least not in a way a bride can win, at all, ever. I had conversations during wedding planning where I would be chided for being spendthrift in the very same breath as I was chided for planning a wedding that was too casual. Add to that the fact that the people chatting with me didn't know me from Adam but felt comfortable offering me opinions. Brides-to-be (like mothers-to-be) are perceived as a special kind of public property, which can be stressful to realize as some stranger is rattling off nonsense advice. Some people deal with this by shutting down problem conversations before they start; others try to reason with people, but some might snap and get angry. Bridezilla angry.

Which brings me to the madness that is the term "bridezilla." You're getting married. You're allowed to care about that. It's okay to be excited. You should feel empowered to decisively make choices that are right for you. Yes, you do have to treat people with respect and are not allowed to mindlessly boss people around (see the etiquette discussion in Chapter 3), but I suspect you're not doing that in the first place. So realize that as a woman in charge of planning a large event, you might get accused of being controlling. You might get called a bridezilla. And that is not your issue. That's the issue of the person who feels at liberty to call you something really offensive.

Sometimes wedding planning can feel lose-lose. You're put in a very high-stress situation where the rules seem rigged, and then, when you get stressed, you're perceived as a bad bride. But you're not a bad bride. You're one person trying to throw an event that keeps everyone happy, while you go through a major life transition. You're allowed to have opinions and make decisions. You're even allowed to get angry now and then. Why? You're the one getting married, and that gives you a few rights, along with all the responsibilities.

Cold Feet

What happens when you realize that you're planning a wedding but you're unsure about actually getting married? Committing to a lifetime with one person is a huge thing. Sometimes the hugeness of it gets lost under the piles of to-do lists, bridesmaid dresses, and drafts of the wedding budget. Sometimes it gets lost under the modern idea that when you already live together, not that much is going to change after getting married. Sometimes it's a panic that pulls us back to reality: getting married is a huge commitment, and not one to be taken lightly.

Forever Is . . . Terrifying

If you're freaking out about getting married, it's important to take a moment to untangle the issues (something you might want to also consider doing is premarital counseling, either alone or with your partner). It's important to differentiate between "I'm not sure I want to marry this person" and "Hoo-boy. Marriage is scary." If some part of you is scared of the forever nature of marriage and the possibility of divorce, this is natural. Before you walk down the aisle, it's important to acknowledge that divorce happens, and may have happened in your family.

It's easy for divorce to become the scary bogeyman in the corner, and for your fear of it to grow, as you avoid facing and talking about it. But divorce is a realistic (if not ideal) possible outcome in marriage, and it needs to be discussed. Kimberly Eclipse was immobilized with anxiety leading up to her wedding and said, "For me, so much of being engaged was just about being brave. It was about being fully aware of the realities of marriage and signing up anyway, knowing that when the time comes I'll fight for my relationship." So if you're scared about divorce, consider it a healthy reaction. Talk about it. Talk to your partner, talk to your parents, talk to any religious figures you might have in your life. Talk to your friends. And stop thinking there is something wrong with you because you're scared.

Calling Off Your Wedding (You Will Survive)

What happens when you figure out that you have something a bit more serious than cold feet? If you realize you're just not sure you want to get married to your partner, slow everything down. Sara Downey called off her wedding just three weeks before it was due to take place. She advised, "Wedding planning is hectic and fast and harried and full of pressure from all kinds of places. Make sure you're actually interested in the 'getting married' bit of the wedding planning—that you want your relationship to have a forever home. Maybe you do. Maybe things are just moving too fast. That's all fine. Just take the time to be sure." If you are really questioning your relationship, now is the time to seek professional help. Get someone to talk to, and start sorting things out in a safe environment.

Though it seems terrifying and expensive to call off a wedding, it is infinitely worse to call off a marriage. If you decide to pull the plug on your wedding, talk to your partner and your family, and then have someone you love and trust sit down with you and draw up a step-by-step plan of what needs to be done. Figure out who can assist you in making those difficult phone calls, and accept all the help you can get. Even though calling off your wedding may seem like the single scariest decision you've ever had to make, you will survive it. You will grieve, you will cry, but by being honest about your needs, you'll have a chance to find what you really want in life. Sara had a really important reminder: "The people who loved you before you were a bride-to-be will still love you once you call off your wedding. I was surprised when my dad told me he doesn't care if I ever get married, as long as I'm happy." No matter what books and movies tell us, getting married does not equal happiness. Getting married *to the right person* gives you a serious shot at happiness.

Forever Is . . . Now

It's also possible that you're not worried about divorce but are instead panicking as you try to wrap your head around the idea of forever. And of course we freak out when we ponder questions like "How long is forever?" and "What if we don't get along in thirty years?" Those questions scare us because they don't have an answer, no matter how long we think about them, and there is nothing we can do to solve the problems they pose. They are, in a sense, totally useless (but terrifying) questions.

For some reason, I never grappled with cold feet before our wedding day. Fast-forward to our one-year anniversary, and I was freaked out. In the months leading up to that day, I'd ended up in several conversations where people gave me a litany of the terrors of marriage. So I spent the day of our anniversary working myself up into a near panic. What *did* forever mean? And why did it feel so claustrophobic? Sometime during that afternoon, as the freaking out reached its peak, I had a realization: my marriage isn't for forever, my marriage is for today. I suddenly understood what we can do is look around our life and figure out how our relationship is doing right now. If it's good, it's good. If it's not, we can take actions to fix it. But there is nothing that can be done about thirty years from now, other than to take care of each other in this moment.

It's perfectly reasonable to be a little scared about the enormity of commitment, and there are ways to deal with this trepidation. Approach the wedding one moment at a time, try to stay grounded, and focus on why you love your partner enough to make this huge commitment. And for goodness' sake, if you realize you don't want to spend the rest of your life with your affianced, be brave, and call it off.

Your Wedding Is Not an Imposition

In recent years, people have slowly started to treat weddings as impositions. This may be a result of receiving one too many wedding invitations instructing them to wear "only gray and fuchsia" to the reception, or one too many invites mandating that they spend their family vacation for the year on a weeklong wedding trip to Costa Rica. But unless you're doing these things, your wedding is not an imposition.

Did you get that? It's not an imposition on *anyone*. You're not treating your guests as props in your stage event. If you're having a destination wedding, you made sure your immediate family could afford tickets and then let everyone else off the hook from attending. So you shouldn't have to worry about that nonsense, but still, somehow you're worried. People will have to travel, or spend money, or spend time, or do something slightly outside their comfort zone, and you're not sure if you're within your rights to ask them to do that.

Your wedding is not an imposition, not because your guests will have fun at your wedding (though they will), but because your guests are grown people. Got that? They are *grown-ups*. Your wedding guests are adults and should be treated as such. They can make their own decisions as to their attendance, they can book their own travel, they can buy you gifts on their own, they can pick their own clothes. And because they made every single one of these decisions on their own, you are not imposing on them in any way. Your wedding is a party that they are delighted to attend. If your wedding is too expensive, or too far away, or just too much of a bother? They won't come. Hopefully, they'll be kind about it when they tell you they can't come. But if they are not, you probably didn't want them there in the first place. Marisa-Andrea Moore Shelby, who got married in a small ceremony in her parents' backyard in Southern California, said, "The people who love you and care about you will not feel like your wedding is a burden or an imposition. They will be thrilled that out of all of the people you could have invited, you want *them*." People are coming to your wedding because they love you, and they want an excuse to celebrate this happy event in your life. Your wedding is not an imposition. Your wedding is a joy.

Planning a Wedding When Life Hurts

There are times when life is so hard that planning a wedding can feel utterly frivolous. During a painful moment in our wedding planning, I came across this quote from Elie Wiesel that forever changed my perception of why we have weddings. In his book *A Jew Today* he says, "In our tradition, celebration of life is more important than mourning over the dead. When a wedding procession encounters a funeral procession in the street, the mourners must halt so as to allow the wedding party to proceed. Surely you know what respect we show our dead, but a wedding, symbol of life and renewal, symbol of promise too, takes precedence." At that moment, I realized what every older adult already knows. Weddings are about hope. Weddings are hope for the future, hope for a new generation, and the hope that love and family can win over everything else. Weddings are not more important than life, nor do they stand apart from life, but they represent something bigger than us, something larger than the dress we wear or the flowers we carry. So on the days it seems too hard to go on, too hard to pick out flowers in the face of deep pain, remember the why of weddings. When life leaves us a puddle on the floor, weddings allow us a reason to hope and give us a brief, shining moment in the sun. They allow us to celebrate who we love with the people we love, which is always, always necessary.

Planning When a Loved One Is Seriously Ill

More often than we'd like to think, wedding planning coincides with a loved one's illness or the death of a family member or friend. If you are engaged and you have a parent or close relative who is very ill, the central question is usually: Do you move up the wedding so they can be there for it, or do you keep the wedding plans as they are? I spoke to one bride who had it both ways and was able to offer insight into what each choice was like. She married her husband in a ceremony over her father's hospital bed. A few months after her father died, the couple held another celebration with a wedding dress and a party. She told me that on her wedding day she could only think about how she was about to lose her dad, so it was one of the saddest days of her life. Though she was glad her father was able to see them married, it turned out that their second celebration was necessary because it was just that: a celebration. It allowed her to enjoy her wedding the way her dad would have wanted her to.

There is, of course, no one right answer to how and when to plan your wedding with a dying parent. You, your partner, your family, and your parent will need to decide what option seems best for all of you.

Planning Without a Parent

Part of the enduring myth of wedding planning is that it is one of the great mother-daughter bonding rituals. We've already discussed how even in good mother-daughter relationships, wedding planning can be more fraught and complicated than expected. But this process can be infinitely more difficult if you have a parent who is absent from your life. The challenges are different depending on the situation—your parent may be emotionally unavailable to you, or may be ill and have very little extra energy for wedding planning, or it may be that you have a deceased parent. Each of these cases is hard in different ways and can leave you grieving for what you feel you deserve: a bonding moment with your mother or father.

One bride who had a mother who was unable to support her through the process told me, "Having an emotionally absent parent, for whatever reason, is hard. There's always a chance for a new hurt." She offered important advice: let yourself grieve. It can be hard to feel like you're allowed to grieve the loss of an experience with a parent who is still alive. But if you have a parent who is unable to participate, or if your relationship is strained, accept that as a loss of what you wished for yourself, and allow yourself to cry it out. Then work to take care of yourself and to protect your heart. Maybe this means having a bridesmaid run interference with your parent, or maybe it means working with your partner to reset your expectations to something more realistic. But don't beat yourself up over crying or feeling sad. You're not overreacting; you're grieving a loss.

It's also possible that wedding planning is bringing up a recent physical, not just an emotional, loss. Lynn Schell told me that planning her wedding a few years after her mother died was "a sickening cycle of excitement and joy followed—approximately eight hours later—by overwhelming grief and anger that permeated every step in the planning process." She said, "I just couldn't handle the emotional roller coaster of loving the feeling of being a bride only to be followed by the sheer devastating disappointment that Mom wouldn't be there to play silly games and make a teary-eyed toast. It was like losing her all over again; only again, and again, and again, and again." In this situation, there is no way out but through. Nothing is going to bring your mom or dad back, and coping with the loss while planning your wedding can be enormously difficult.

Lynn told me that what saved her in the end was learning that her partner was not going to understand why she was upset unless she told him. She said, "When I finally gave up hoping he would get it, and finally started saying simply 'I miss my mom' every time I felt it, we got on the same page about how complex and difficult a daughter-sans-mother existence can be." You miss your mom (or dad, or other important person in your life). That's not going to go away. Allow yourself to tell people what you need, even if it's nothing other than a shoulder to cry on, and let them support you.

There Is No Substitute for a Missing Parent (Except, Sometimes There Is)

If one of your parents isn't around to emotionally support you through wedding planning, it's important to realize early on that you can't expect someone to completely fill in for him or her. As Lynn told me, "Your bridesmaids are not your mother. Your groom is not your mother. Your father is not your mother." But when in crisis, get help, even if that means hiring someone. She explains that you need to find "candidates who can be 'mother by proxy,' who you can sit down with and really explain what you need during this time. For me it was unconditional positive affirmations, constant and boundless energy, and the desire to make this the best party ever." Once you realize that no one can step into the void of the missing parent, you can start identifying specific areas where you need help. The bride with the emotionally absent mother told me, "No one can replace your mother—for better or worse, she's your mom. But! People can replace her in tasks that traditionally fall to the mother of the bride. I am lucky, and I have an amazing mother-in-law, who did things like organizing breakfast on the wedding day and talking me off (planning-related) ledges and telling me I looked beautiful." People want to support you, because they know you are dealing with a loss, and because it's your wedding day, damn it. But you need to tell them that you need help, and then tell them exactly what you need. Maybe you need someone to go wedding dress shopping with you, but you know you're going to sob afterward because your mom wasn't there. You know you need someone to pat you on the back for twenty minutes while you cry and then take you out to lunch and make you laugh. Tell them that. People can't guess what your needs are before you figure them out yourself, but you're allowed to tell them how to help, I swear to it.

Have a Wedding

The number-one piece of advice I've received from every single bride dealing with pain while wedding planning is: have a wedding. The power of bringing people together in joy, particularly in a time of sorrow, is power that cannot be underestimated. Caitlin Driscoll Cannon, whose mother-in-law died rather suddenly of cancer the same week as their wedding, said, "I thought we should cancel, but as soon as I uttered the words, a wave of no's from both sides of the family drowned out my hesitations. And so we had a wedding. And that's what mattered. That in the midst of the saddest week of our lives, we were joining our families and friends to say: this is hard, but there is still joy. And we've learned that a wedding is not just 'your day,' it is a day to celebrate the lives you were born into, the ones you've made, the ones you continue to build."

Even when not dealing with a death in the family, weddings can be emotionally difficult. As much as society at large acts like planning a wedding is a carefree romp, the reality is often far more difficult. We're forced to talk with people we love about the big issues: belief, money, and friendship. We're negotiating a

THE PRACTICAL BRIDE REMEMBERS . . .

- The hardest part of wedding planning is often the conflict between what we hoped would be, and what is. Dealing with this can be painful and emotional.

- A major component of the engagement process is learning to set boundaries between your family of origin and your brand-new-baby family. If you find yourself fighting with family, think of it as bringing you a little closer to a new form of family harmony.

- Planning a major event with your partner is going to help you develop skills for working together that you'll use for years. In the meantime, however, things might feel a little tricky.

- Getting married is stressful, crazy, and exciting. You're allowed to experience all of these emotions and call the shots in your own wedding planning, without anyone calling you a bridezilla.

- Actually committing to someone for the rest of your life can be terrifying. If you find yourself struggling with cold feet, try to figure out whether you're scared by the idea of "forever" or you're not sure you want to marry your partner. If it's the latter, slow everything down. Calling off a wedding is a heck of a lot easier than calling off a marriage.

- Your wedding is not an imposition. Grown-ups can make their own decisions about attending your wedding, and how they will celebrate with you. Kids will enjoy the cake and punch, regardless.

- If you're dealing with difficult emotions when planning, tell people exactly what kind of help you need, and let them emotionally support you.

- Weddings represent hope, love, and the resilience of the human spirit. If there is any time we need this kind of celebration, it's in the face of the really hard stuff.

gathered. You're vowing to spend your life with another person, and that's huge. So give it the attention it deserves, whether you are writing it from scratch or merely making adjustments to a traditional service.

Think of it this way: if you create a really meaningful wedding ceremony, you can put less effort into the rest of the party.

A PRACTICAL BRIDE SPEAKS
A Theological Scottish Wedding
BY CLARE ADAMA

On our wedding day, I was really surprised at how much I enjoyed myself. I thought that the day would be meaningful, but not the kind of day I would really enjoy, because I'm just not "bride material." I'm goofy and nerdy, and the things I like best are laughing very hard, tea, silly dancing, and good conversation with friends—that is, nothing beautiful or serene. So I feel slightly awkward saying this, but September 12, 2009, was the best day of my life.

It was the best day because in the morning, I spent time drinking tea with my closest friends. I spent time with my mum laughing at my hair in rollers. I took a walk with my dad and heard him say how proud he was. I listened to music written and performed by our talented friends. I took part in a ceremony that was in equal parts joyful, meaningful, inclusive, and downright hilarious. I sat in my family home drinking tea with my husband and best man. I saw my friends reading and talking about books that I love. I ate sausage and mash and awesome banoffee pie. I saw my bridesmaid land a speech that she had been so nervous about. I danced in stupid and amusing ways with my friends. Any one of these things makes a day good for me. All in one day, well, was I a happy girl. And somewhere in the middle of that, I married my best friend.

In our marriage, we aim to recognize and welcome community; we carry with us and are carried by so many friends and family. So, we tried to have the kind of wedding that represented and communicated this. Rather than me being given away by my family, the whole community gave us to each other. As a married

[continues]

If your guests are on an emotional high after basking in your love and wiping away their tears, they are much less likely to notice that the centerpieces never showed up. So yes, I'm totally making the argument that writing a meaningful ceremony is the lazy girl's way of avoiding too much focus on the details of the reception.

couple we made promises to the community, and they to us. We tried to ensure that our guests were participants rather than spectators and that they felt welcomed and included.

We were aware that whilst we wanted the ceremony to represent what we believe and value, friends and family would be there who hold different faiths, and some with none. We tried to make sure the service was inclusive and participatory, without anyone feeling uncomfortable. We chose readings that reflected on the joyfulness of spirituality, picked up on ideas of community and journey, and used inclusive language. Also, the minister marrying us was one of my lecturers and an old family friend, and did a brilliant job of making the ceremony relaxed, personal, and welcoming.

Some of the most meaningful compliments were from those who appreciated how much effort we had put into making them feel welcome and part of the day. It particularly meant a lot to have friends who were usually very uncomfortable in religious settings say that they really enjoyed the service and found it very meaningful. Some also commented on how much they appreciated that it made them feel like participants whilst not forcing our beliefs upon them.

We weren't really aiming for either a traditional or nontraditional wedding. We thought about what was meaningful to us and our friends and family, and how to represent that on the day, as well as what was going to be best logistically. In actual fact, we started with our guest list and worked from there. So here's the thing—whether you are planning a traditional or nontraditional, typical or atypical wedding. Ask yourself: Whose tradition is this anyway? I consider tradition something that should provide nourishment and challenge to us on emotional and spiritual levels; it is a place where we can belong and can ask our questions.

Maybe you're constructing a ceremony from scratch, or maybe you're having a traditional service. In this chapter we'll discuss ways of making the service meaningful, selecting an officiant, and thinking about the vows you'll make. And finally we'll dive into the big question: How will it feel? Maybe it will feel gritty, maybe transcendent, maybe like nothing much, but probably totally surprising.

Issues of Faith

Your beliefs are the fundamental building blocks of your ceremony, whether they are religious or secular. Perhaps you, your partner, and your family share a cohesive set of values. If not, well, join the club. Discovering the realities of what you and your loved ones hold as truth is part of the reason you go through the engagement process. You are starting a brand-new family, and it's important to start figuring out what your values are, even when that's complicated.

Secular Versus Religious

You would think that the choice between a secular and a religious wedding would be an easy one. "We go to church!" "We don't go to church!" Done.

You would be wrong.

Questions of faith in families are complicated, and weddings often bring up deep-seated issues. Your parents may not have darkened the door of a church since your baptism, and suddenly insist that they are deeply religious people and your wedding will not be valid if it's not in a church. Tricky.

So what do you do? First, talk to your partner. Your first responsibility is to the spiritual life of the family you are going to create. Don't start your married life on a foundation of something you think is false. If the idea of a religious wedding is anathema to either you or your partner, you need to have a conversation with your parents. You need to explain to them that the wedding is the first part of defining your new family's traditions and ethics; religion and/or God is not going to have a place in the spiritual life of your family, but you still love and respect their choices. This conversation is not going to be an easy one. But you need to have this conversation at some point, and sooner is better than later.

Second, stay flexible. Maybe you and your partner are not personally active in your parents' faith, but honoring their cultural legacy is important to you. If so, be open to that. Christen Karle Muir was initially upset at her parents' insistence that her wedding take place in a Catholic church but in the end came to terms with it. She said, "At first it frustrated me that my parents would not budge, but I understood their position—it is their faith and my upbringing and I am grateful for it. I am spiritual in my own way and use tools from a Catholic foundation to create my own multifaceted, nondenominational approach to the mysteries of life. Nonetheless, I am inescapably a Catholic at heart. Life, love, and the spirit are complicated, and this is who I am." For many of us, grappling with faith issues during wedding planning allows us a chance to make peace with what we believe and why. That's a gift (even if it feels painful at the time).

Interfaith Weddings

If you and your partner don't share a faith background, you have the advantage of any conflict being right out in the open. Though I know this doesn't always make you feel lucky, try to embrace it. There are wedding books that will tell you that having an interfaith wedding is exciting and easy because you have two whole faiths to choose from (lucky you!). As someone who had an interfaith wedding, I can tell you this is a bit of an . . .

idealistic take on things. Dealing with two faith systems is complicated and deserves a book of its own (see Selected Sources for some recommendations), but it's almost never easy.

If you haven't had a long talk about your personal values systems and how those intersect with your personal religious practices, now is the time to do that. What values do you share? Where do your beliefs differ? Don't avoid the places where you disagree, as those conversations can provide a rich and complex foundation for your marriage. Then move on to a discussion of your religious backgrounds, and how you want them to shape your family life and your wedding service. Do you want an interfaith service, or a service of just one faith? Remember, there is no right answer to this question, and thoughtful disagreement might unearth fascinating things about how your partner thinks about religion. If you decide you want an interfaith service, explore the realities of what that might look like. Will your religious leaders officiate an interfaith service? Will your families of origin be comfortable with this kind of service? The key is to strike a balance between something that works for each of you and something that makes sense in the context of your religious beliefs. If you begin a conversation about faith and religion that you'll continue for the rest of your life, that's wedding planning time well spent.

Finding an Officiant

Once you've decided on the basic faith constructs of your wedding, it's time to find an officiant. If you're having a religious ceremony, your options may be somewhat constrained. If you're having a secular ceremony, your options may be terrifyingly wide-open. But the most basic question you should ask yourselves about any officiant is simply: Do I like this person? Do I, on a gut level, want him or her to usher me into the institution of marriage? If you don't, move on. If you do, here are some questions to help you start a dialogue with your potential officiant:

- Will you work with us to help construct a ceremony/ select readings and music that make the ceremony meaningful to us?

- Will you provide premarital counseling? If not, can you provide a list of books about marriage that would be helpful for us to read and discuss?

- Can you tell us about wedding ceremonies that you performed that you found particularly moving?

- Are you comfortable with the elements we are planning for our ceremony? (If not, why not? Sometimes what you learn will change your mind.)

- What is your definition of marriage?

- Will you work with us to create vows or to find a way to make the traditional vows meaningful to us?

- What do you wear when you perform a wedding?

- Will you help guide us through the time before our service? What thoughts do you have on helping couples enter the service in a grounded and focused way? (Translation: If I totally freak out before I walk down the aisle, are you going to pat me on the back and tell me to breathe? Because you'd better.)

- Do you stay after the service and socialize at the reception? Why or why not?

- Or, if you're asking a friend to perform your service, ask: Is this something you are comfortable doing? Why would you like to officiate for us?

Once you've met with one or two (or six) officiants and asked some of the above questions, sit down with your partner and focus on the most important questions of all: Who do you like? Who do you trust? Who do you want standing next to you when you say your vows? Let that guide your selection. And if you have very limited choices because of your faith, remember, it's wonderful to work with a practiced officiant within a tradition that's had meaning for thousands of years.

Constructing Your Own Ceremony

Writing a ceremony can seem exciting and liberating, while feeling terrifying and overwhelming at the exact same time. So start by building a foundation. Caitlin Helms, who was married in Duluth, Minnesota, said, "Before you write a ceremony, I think you need to figure out what you believe about marriage fundamentally." Take this opportunity to discuss what marriage means to you. Once you've figured that out, let it stand as a mission statement for your ceremony.

Here is the closely guarded secret of writing a wedding service: you don't really need to write your ceremony from scratch. In fact, it may be impossible to write it from scratch. After all, you're choosing to join an institution with a history that spans thousands of years. Chances are, you're not going to reinvent the wheel. So realize that part of what's beautiful about marriage is its universality, and take some pressure off yourself to create the perfect, personalized service. You're just trying to create something that's honest.

Start by looking for a service structure that reflects your basic views about what marriage is. Maybe it's the Episcopal wedding liturgy, or the civil ceremony as performed in your country; maybe it's something you find farther afield. Just find something that has a ring of truth for you. Once you have picked the frame that you'll use to structure your service, discover your relationship to it. As you look at the ceremony, there are probably going to be bits that each of you dislike, and other parts that one or the other of you finds very important. You may be surprised what parts of the service get an emotional reaction from one or both of you. So be careful with yourself and go slowly. Take out things that don't work. If you have a really strong emotional reaction to something, try to figure out why. That will help you shape your service (and marriage) and help you discover how close or how far you want to be from your particular version of tradition.

Once you've ironed out a basic service structure, it's time to consider adding in things you love. If you ask me, this is the fun part. Collect a list of readings and music that you might want to use, and start fitting them into your structure. From here, tweak, adjust, play, polish. Consider how long you want the service to be, or how short. Question assumptions: Does the bride have to walk down the aisle? Do either of you have to walk down the aisle? Heck, do you want an aisle in the first place? Whatever you do, remember to keep a sense of play.

Making a Traditional Ceremony Your Own

You're getting married in a house of worship, or you're having a standard civil ceremony, and you're going to celebrate your wedding with time-honored traditions. Excellent. First, let's dispel the popular myth that traditional ceremonies are boring. If a traditional service is part of who you are, then that service is going to be emotional and personal and real. There is no quicker way to make a ceremony boring than to have the couple think it's a little dull, so let go of that idea right now.

When you're working within the confines of a more traditional service, think of the age-old structure as a vessel. It's something you're going to fill up with emotion, with your personalities, with family, and with the love you have for each other. And the older the service, the stronger the vessel.

So, how do you fill up your wedding service? How do you take a bunch of words that you didn't pick and make them your own? Here are some ideas:

- Intention. Why are you having a traditional wedding in the first place? Maybe it's important to you personally. Maybe it's significant to your parents, and you've realized that honoring them is a key part of who you are. Whatever the reasons, think about it, and talk it through with your partner.

- What does it all mean? Next, start looking at the service together. It's really easy to gloss over words you've heard a million times, but stop doing that. Look at the words of your service and talk about them. What do they mean to each of you personally? If your wedding service just seems like a bunch of boring words to you, it's going to put your guests to sleep. If your wedding service is a bunch of really meaningful and specific words, you'll make your guests cry.

- Thoughtfully add music and readings. Almost all traditional services have room for you to add and subtract readings and music. When the bulk of your service is set, it's important to really think about your choices. Religious and time-honored texts and musical traditions have so much rich and amazing material to choose from, you could spend a lifetime picking.

- Value your choices. Stop writing off your wedding as "boring" or "traditional." If you fill up the vessel of tradition with yourselves, I'm pretty sure that's as good as it can possibly get.

- Show up. If you show up, if you're fully emotionally present, if you've thought carefully about the choices you've made? Well. I'll be the girl in the back bawling.

Vows: Personal and Traditional

If the ceremony is the core of the wedding, then the core of the service is your vows. This is the moment where you make promises to each other in front of witnesses, and vow to bind your lives together forever. So, you know, no small thing. Take some time to think about the words you're going to say, whether they are traditional or nontraditional. Weigh them on your heart, and let them change you. Whatever you say, make it simple, personal, and yours. Let that be the detail of the wedding that matters and be what you remember forever.

Writing Your Own Vows

Writing your own vows is an excellent opportunity to sit down with your partner, discuss what marriage means for you, and allow that to be reflected in the promises you make. First, ponder what form you want them to take. Do you want them to be a personal discussion of your relationship, or a more universal statement on what marriage is to you? Do you want them to be something you write in secret, or something you craft together as a thoughtful statement about your partnership? Lauren Davis Wojtkun, who married in the MIT chapel in Cambridge, had an officiant who told her that his concerns with self-written vows were that they were not usually promises, and that even when they were, often people did not make equal pledges to each other. Because of this, Lauren and her husband worked to construct vows that were one set of promises repeated by each person. Maddie Eisenhart and her husband, who married in a low-key service on a public beach in Maine, each wrote their own vows. They took the form of statements about their shared history, their hopes for the future, and the promises they were making to each other. Vows can come in any number of forms, but I would encourage you to root them in discussion and take your time writing them.

Remember that it's okay to keep things simple. The act of making enormous promises to another person is, in itself, a statement of love. Vows do not always need to be in the form of a love letter to another person; they can be short, or simple pledges. And try not to pressure yourself to make jokes. There is a time and place for jokes at a wedding: during the toasts, when everyone is a little tipsy. Let your ceremony be a place for un-varnished truth, for digging deep and speaking about what is really important to you. As Maddie Eisenhart told me, "Nothing is going to make your vows as powerful as really saying, quite simply, why the hell it is you're getting married." Whatever you write, let it be a statement of your core values, of what you believe your marriage to be.

Time-Honored Vows

If you're getting married in a religious setting, chances are that you'll be required to use time-honored vows. Or perhaps you have been thinking about writing your vows and can't quite get comfortable with it. If that's the case, I'm going to toss this idea out there: don't. Getting married means joining in a tradition that is thousands of years old. By saying the same words that generations and generations before you have said, you tie yourselves to the strength of an institution that has stood the test of time, helped people survive great hardships, and helped them embrace enormous joy. Like a traditional ceremony, your vows will have emotion and meaning if you think about them, and discuss them, and know what you're saying and why. The timelessness of the words you say will only add power.

A Moment of Transcendence

I would describe the thirty-minute process of actually getting married as transcendent, in a literal way. The definition of transcendent is "extending or lying beyond the limits of ordinary experience," or "being beyond the limits of all possible experience and knowledge." Our wedding ceremony was not the happiest moment of my life, nor was it perfect. I didn't feel like a fairy princess; I didn't even tear up much. Instead it felt gritty and raw. It felt like something I'd never experienced before and like something I probably will never experience again. It felt outside the bounds of ordinary experience. In the end, all I can say is that I felt different walking down the aisle than I felt walking back up. So for me, getting married was transcendent, but not in a glowy, magical way. Anna Shapiro said, "Transcendent moments are not about perfection or joy, or fairy tales coming to fruition; rather, they're about moments of powerful realization about the world that we are a part of and forces that are much bigger than us." And that is what a thoughtful wedding service can do. It can tie us to the greater human experience, and to a larger institution. There is power in making huge commitments in front of a community of witnesses (whether

THE PRACTICAL BRIDE REMEMBERS . . .

- The ceremony is where you do the really important bit: get married. So give it the attention it deserves, whether you're writing a ceremony from scratch or making small adjustments to a traditional service.

- The fundamental building blocks of your ceremony are your beliefs. Take time to discuss them, whether religious or secular, with your partner. Don't avoid disagreements. They can be a rich foundation for your marriage.

- When looking for an officiant, remember that you want to find someone you like, on a gut level. This person will be ushering you into the institution of marriage.

- When writing a ceremony, start by discussing what marriage means to you. Next, look for an existing structure that you can modify to reflect your beliefs.

- If you're using a traditional service, think about why this service is meaningful to you, and approach it with intention and emotion. If you do this, your ceremony will be anything but boring.

- When writing your own vows, allow time to craft something simple and meaningful. When using traditional vows, consider the power of saying the same words as the many generations that have gone before you.

- Once you've crafted your ceremony, show up emotionally.

A Snow in August Wedding

BY ANNA MAHONY

We got married on August 15 and had planned an awesome barbecue picnic on a ranch in a meadow by a lake in the Colorado mountains. Think ribs, potato salad, home-brewed beer, and apple pie, followed by an epic dance party. Nice, right?

I say "had planned" because all of that didn't actually happen. Why? Well, two hours before the ceremony was set to start, it began raining. Then an hour later the temperature dropped to 37 degrees and it started hailing and snowing. Did we have a Plan B? Nope. We'd planned pretty much everything except a Plan B because it's usually 95 degrees and hot as h-e-double-hockey-sticks during this time of year. Snow? That wasn't on our wedding radar. No way, no sir.

So. Our guests were set to arrive in fifteen minutes, and as Mike and I watched torrential rain blow chairs over and tablecloths away, we let go of the wedding we'd worked to plan for so many months. We decided to move the whole shindig up the hill to an old barn and hoped for the best. The most important thing was that we got married that day, and we were going to Do It Or Else.

But here is where things got good. Here is when our wedding actually happened. Because when the guests arrived and saw us— wearing jeans and rain slickers—moving food, supplies, and tables up a muddy hill in the rain, they got to work. They created an assembly line to get chairs up to the second floor of the barn for the ceremony. Mike's brother brought the car over and started bumping Michael Jackson. The caterers moved all their equipment inside, set up the bar, and started passing whiskey around to warm everyone up. People hung lights, lit candles, and set up jars of flowers (that were supposed to be for the tables) all over the place.

I'll remember everyone laughing, helping, and pitching in as some of the most wonderful moments of my life. Despite the rain and the mud and the cold, everyone had a fantastic time. I think it's actually pretty amazing that the universe rained on our wedding parade. It encouraged me to let go, to sit back and focus on what was really happening—that all our favorite people were together in one place and that I was promising to spend the rest of my life with my very best friend. At that moment I was able to see that our wedding couldn't possibly go wrong because the most important things were so very right.

ten hours and experience them to their fullest? How do we get what we need out of this transitional moment and move forward with minimal regrets and a lifetime of memories?

To start, show up emotionally. Let go of all the planning you worked so hard on, and embrace imperfection. That sounds gauzy and hippie-Zen and impossible, right? Well, it's really none of those things. In this chapter we'll lay the groundwork for the day itself: strategies for organizing the event, creating spreadsheets and timelines, asking for help, and then handing all of that work to a wedding stage manager (or anyone who is not you). Once you've done all that, we'll discuss how to move from the planning to the doing. We'll tackle managing family drama, and learning when to let go of all the stress and stay present. And finally, we'll discover how weddings are impossible to ruin, which is less crazy than it sounds.

Your Day-Of Spreadsheet

The funny thing about wedding planning is that when it starts, it feels like it's all about pretty things. But when you are finally down to the wire, wedding planning has nothing to do with style and everything to do with hauling. Who is getting the beer to the picnic site? Who is transporting the decorations to the venue? Who is bringing the leftover flowers home? A successful wedding plan is not about picking out the perfect centerpiece; it's about making sure the centerpieces land on the tables.

In Chapter 5, we talked about creating a variety of spreadsheets to help with wedding planning, but the most important document of them all is the day-of spreadsheet. Having a spreadsheet that outlines your wedding day in exquisite, painstaking detail may seem like a bananas-stressful way to fill your time prewedding. But trust me, this document will be the one you treasure above all others. It will be the one you hand over to your wedding stage manager. It will be what makes the day flow smoothly, and the one that allows you to fully let go

Time	Activity	Location	Person In Charge
10:30am	Ceremony starts	Venue - Outdoors	—
11:00am	Ceremony ends	Venue - Outdoors	—
11:00am	Yichud	Venue - Indoors	Meg & David
11:00am	Cocktail hour starts	Venue - Outdoors	—
11:00am	Polaroid duty	Venue - Indoors	Rachel, Wade, Amanda, Gabby
11:00am	Playlist monitor & Sound tech	Venue - Indoors	Kevin
11:00am	MC	Venue - Indoors	Emily
11:15am	A few couple pictures	Venue - Outdoors	Meg, David, photographers
11:20am	Meg & David join cocktails	Venue - Outdoors	Meg & David
11:45am	Toasts begin	Venue - Indoors	Stan, Various
Noon	Lunch is served	Venue - Indoors	—
12:45pm	Cake cutting	Venue - Indoors	Meg & David
12:50pm	First dance	Venue - Indoors	Meg & David
1:00pm	DANCE PARTY	Venue - Indoors	—
1:35pm	Chair dance	Venue - Indoors	Meg & David
1:45pm	Mezinka	Venue - Indoors	Anita & Stan
1:50pm	Hora	Venue - Indoors	—
2:00pm	DANCE PARTY, cont'd.	Venue - Indoors	—
2:40pm	Last dance	Venue - Indoors	Meg & David
2:45pm	Send-off	Venue - Outdoors	Meg, David, Kate
3:00pm	Party is over	Venue - Indoors	—
3:00pm	Flowers/Leftovers given out	Venue - Indoors	Kate, Caterers
3:00pm	Presents/Wine/Ritual items taken home	Venue - Indoors	Both families
3:00pm	Sound system struck	Venue - Indoors	Kevin, Kory
3:30pm	Items transported to Meg & David's apartment	Truck	Kate, Kevin Rachel, Wade

and absorb the experience of getting married, knowing there is a good plan in competent hands.

Above is a sample spreadsheet based on our wedding day. It's divided into four columns: time, activity, location, and person in charge. I have included just the section of our spreadsheet pertaining to the reception, but I encourage you to do equally detailed planning for the whole day, and perhaps for the day before as well.

We set precise times for how the wedding day was supposed to unfold, with the full knowledge that things would change or fall behind schedule. We assembled a team of helpers and assigned them to specific tasks. Sometimes they worked individually, and sometimes they worked in teams. In all cases we asked people to help out under the direction of our wedding stage manager. She was the one who made sure everything got done and made judgment calls about particular problems. She moved the day along from one event to the next, so that David and I could focus on the emotional and spiritual aspects of the day instead of the logistics.

Our day-of spreadsheet also included a few other tabs. We called one of our tabs "prop management." That was how we tracked the important family heirlooms used that day. It wouldn't do to have these tremendously important items get lost, so we assigned each one to a responsible family member for safekeeping. We also had an all-important contacts tab, so that our wedding stage manager had everything she needed. This way, as problems arose she could make phone calls herself.

Having all this information collected in one place may feel like a real pain during the lead-up to your wedding. But this kind of organization allows you to step back and become a bride, relinquishing the role of event manager to someone else. This will prove a key part of preserving your ability to fully experience your wedding day.

One word of warning: though it's important to plan what your helpers will be doing on your wedding day, don't even think of planning for your guests. Sara Hilliard Garratt, who got married after a four-day celebration in a nature reserve in South Africa, put it this way: "Don't try to micromanage your guests. Most of them are grown-ups (and the children are even harder to organize). Micromanaging might be appreciated by a grand total of five people, but on the whole, guests probably couldn't be bothered: they'll do what makes them happy in the context of celebrating your marriage." The modern wedding industry occasionally has the bad idea of treating wedding guests like props in a production: Have them stand here! Tell them to wear pink and black! Make them open party favors in unison! The fact is, your wedding guests are adults. They've been going to weddings for a long time (many of them since well before you were born), and they have a general idea of how to comport themselves. Allow them to do so.

Your Day-Of Timeline

The average wedding timeline given in most planning handbooks is five and a half hours: half an hour for the ceremony, five hours for the reception. This is not always realistic, and it's certainly not traditional. If your reception isn't going to be five hours long, it will be long enough. And if you're partying long into the night, you'll want to plan for that, too.

No matter the length of your reception, it's worth it to plan the pacing and order of events. Successful entertaining is all about timing: feeding people when they are hungry, and having one activity flow relatively seamlessly into the next. The more you're coloring outside the wedding lines, the more important it is for guests to feel taken care of. As long as you make it clear what is happening next, they will go with the flow and most likely will not even notice what you left out. Joy (mixed with organization) has a delightful way of blurring memories.

With that in mind, let's talk through things you might want to include on your wedding day timeline (though obviously none of these things are mandatory). Once you create an outline for the day, you can turn it over to your wedding stage manager and know that the things that are most important to you will (probably) happen. Keep in mind: it's a wedding. Things are going to run late. Plan for that.

PREWEDDING ACTIVITIES

- Getting ready: This can be together or apart.

- Spending quality time with friends and family: This is a nice way to spend the day if you are having an afternoon or evening reception.

- Venue setup: Try to outsource as much of this as you can to friends, loved ones, and/or professionals.

- Pictures: The more pictures you can take before the wedding starts, the more time you have to celebrate.

- A first look: If you don't get ready together but want to see each other before the ceremony, you might want to set up a formal first-look moment with your photographer.

- Getting to the venue: Make sure to schedule a realistic amount of time for this, accounting for traffic.

CEREMONY-RELATED ACTIVITIES

- Preceremony formalities: For example, a ketubah signing, or any other traditions that are part of your cultural heritage.

- Processional: Make sure you allow time to get lined up and grounded before you walk down the aisle. Also, remember that you can opt out of a processional altogether, if you so choose.

- Ceremony: Guests tend to run late, so plan on starting your ceremony at least fifteen minutes after the time listed on your invitation.

- Receiving line: An official and traditional (but not mandatory) way to greet guests.

- *Yichud:* Jewish tradition requires that the couple take fifteen minutes alone together immediately after the ceremony. This can be a wonderful way to soak in the enormity of what just happened, even for non-Jewish couples.

- If you have a legal marriage license, remember to sign it!

RECEPTION ACTIVITIES

- Cocktail hour.

- A group photo of you and all your guests.

- Wedding party photos: Hint: if you delay your guests eating so you can take hours of pictures, you will make them very cranky.

- Couple photos: Even if you take the bulk of your photos before the ceremony, taking five minutes of photos together when you're giddy from your vows can be wonderful. Consider taking more extensive photos before or after the reception, or even the next day.

- A grand entrance as a married couple: Very optional. Feel free to just wander into your reception if that's more your style.

- Toasts: As many or as few as you'd like, made by whoever is important to you.

- Food: This can mean serving a meal or serving snacks.

- Greeting of guests: Some couples formally make the rounds to say hello, which can be a nice alternative to a receiving line.

- Cutting a cake or other dessert.

- A first dance: This can happen before or after food.

- A family dance, a father/daughter dance, a mother/son dance.

- General dancing.

- Any ceremonial dances (the hora, etc.).

- Bouquet and/or garter toss.

- A non-dancing social activity, like board games.

- A preorganized send-off.

A Wedding Stage Manager

Though you may not have a wedding planner (and you don't need a wedding planner), you're not going to do this alone. Period. Every time you get the bright idea that maybe you don't really need help, walk over to the mirror and tell yourself calmly but firmly, "Yes, I actually do."

Wedding planning is really different from getting married. Or as Sharon Hsu, who married in a Presbyterian church in Atlanta, said, "Planning the wedding was hard; getting married wasn't." Planning your wedding is like planning any other event. There are contracts to be signed, details to be worked out, a day (or more) to be scheduled, and stuff to be transported. But on the wedding day itself, you need to find a way to transform yourself from she-who-planned into she-who-is-tying-the-knot. Don't even think of trying to do both. Brides who try to run the show while getting married often turn into stressed-out and screamy brides. Attempting to do both at once is like trying to be the stage manager of a play you're starring in. Or worse, it's like trying to be the stage manager for a potentially life-changing experience. You can't be worried about whether the caterer put the table numbers out when you're busy tying your life to that of another person.

So what is the solution? I suggest picking a friend who will help you with day-of coordination, and calling this wonderful person a wedding stage manager. I like this term because it's no-nonsense, and it conveys the important task of the day: making sure it all gets done. A stage manager: nothing more, nothing less.

If you feel uncomfortable asking a friend for a no-strings-attached favor, consider asking a friend for a trade. Sara Hilliard Garratt explained, "Some people love to organize things. I know this because I'm one of them. Find those people. Use them, but insist that they don't stress. They will love it." Don't force stage-managing on your most disorganized friend. You will be more stressed instead of less, and she will feel that she's disappointed you. Find your friend who is super organized and secretly loves running things. Ask her to help, and tell her that you in no way expect perfection. If she gives you the gift of her organization for the day, and you give her the gift of your trust, things will work out well. Or well enough, and that's generally what we're aiming for.

And when it comes down to it, if you don't have someone you can ask to help, for goodness' sake, hire a day-of coordinator. You are not failing as a laid-back bride if you get someone

to help you out. Sometimes there is simplicity in paying someone to manage logistics for you, or it's worth it to have a hired
authority figure to tell your mom to chill out. When hiring a
wedding planner, make sure you share a philosophy and that
you like her. And make her read this book, so you're both on
the same laid-back page.

Asking for More Help (Yes, You Need It)

I'll say it again: unless you are honest-to-God eloping, you will
need help. And in this era of highly personal, very professional
weddings, this can be tricky. When we asked our friends to help
on our wedding day—to do things like help set up the flowers
the morning of, or help man our DJ station—some people said
no. More than that, people were slightly confused to be asked.
Aren't weddings parties where you just show up? Why would we
ask them to help? But with some explaining and many prom-
ised drinks, people stepped up. "I learned that some friends,
while they mean the best, really just won't come through when
you need them to, which can be kind of heart-breaking," said
Emily Gutman, a wedding photographer who married on California's central coast. "I also learned that other friends, who you
don't think you can count on, so you don't even bother asking,
will surprise you with support, or manual labor, when you least
expect it." And it's the people who do show up, who lift things,
solve last-minute problems, and fix your makeup when you cry
who imbue your wedding day with an unexpected richness. It's
those people who make the whole process worth it.

Some people are good at weddings. In fact, some normally
flaky friends will stun you with how much they care about
your wedding. But other close friends? They might be horrible
at weddings. Maybe they have never planned one, and they
don't know what it's like. Or maybe they are introverts who
hate big parties or are uncomfortable with the idea of marriage

in general. If you end up having friends who don't help you out or don't support you during planning, remember this: some people are terrible at weddings but phenomenal at other things—like exchanging girl-gossip and making you laugh when you're feeling blue. And that's okay. But remember, after asking for help, it is equally important that you let people give it in their own way. You allow your family and friends to love you when you let them help. It turns out that weddings have their own magic, and many people want to be part of that. People want to lift you up. Your job is to let them.

Maintaining Control: The "I'm Going to F*cking Kill You" Moment

We tend to think that on our wedding day everyone will be on his or her best behavior. And they will, sort of. But you know how your loved ones act in high-stress situations? You know how your mom freaks out on Thanksgiving about having the table set just right, and you have a brother who's super delight-ful but slightly socially awkward in large groups, and you have two girlfriends who don't really get along that well after the four glasses of wine they always insist on having? Yeah. That stuff is going to happen on your wedding day, because weddings are stressful. The secret is, it doesn't have to matter.

Being a bride has certain perks—one of which is being given a free pass to not give a shit. More specifically, you're al-lowed to think, "I'm going to f*cking kill you!" and then to think, "You know what? I'm getting married right now; this is not my problem," and turn around and walk away.

You're not going to be able to make everyone happy on your wedding day, and that's fine. Keeping everyone happy is not your job. For ten hours of your life, your job is to protect your own experience; your job is to refuse to get emotionally in-volved when people get stressed. It's tricky to just walk away and let it go, but your wedding celebration only lasts for a few short hours. Tomorrow you can get totally pissed at your mom when she starts berating your sister in front of your guests, but for today, it's not your problem.

You're probably going to have some moments of serious stress during your wedding weekend. Many of us have an "I'm going to f*cking kill you!" moment during the week of our wedding. That moment does not mean you are not having the proper bridal experience. It may just mean that you're paying attention to your surroundings and are calm enough to notice when people are acting crazy.

The Emotional Bodyguard

You already have a wedding stage manager, but depending on the state of affairs in your family when the stress ratchets up, you might also want to consider getting an emotional body-guard (and maybe giving your difficult stepmother one as well). Before you get married, you think that bridesmaids exist to look pretty and throw you a bridal shower. Well, that's not quite it. Bridesmaids exist to stand in front of the bride on her wedding day, and not let crazy within ten feet. Even if you don't have bridesmaids, it might be a good idea to have a friend or two ap-pointed to do this emotional-bodyguard work. And yes, if you have a slightly irrational family member, assign someone who knows her well to the job of steering her away from the huge ar-gument she was about to launch into.

Or maybe all of your friends and family are eminently sane, deeply reasonable, and never show signs of wear and tear under stress.

Maybe.

But you might want to appoint an emotional bodyguard just in case.

Letting Go: The "F*ck It" Moment

So, you had your "I'm going to f*cking kill you" moment. Maybe you even stayed up a little extra late on the night before your wedding, enumerating the people you would like to go jump in a lake, and wondering if this made you a bad bride. Or maybe you had a calm night's sleep, with no stress, and woke up in a cloud of pink rose petals. Or maybe you were somewhere in between. Regardless, on your wedding day, you will move from the planning to the doing. To make this transition, you need to have your "f*ck it" moment.

At some point on your wedding day, all that doing must become being. If you have a hard time letting go of stress, I suggest pre-designating your "f*ck it" moment. A good choice is the moment you prepare to put on your wedding dress. You've done your very best to plan your wedding. You've done the emotional preparation for this life transition. It's time to let the rest go. Maybe your flowers are going to turn out just the way you imagined them; maybe they are not. Maybe your family members are going to be delightful; maybe they are going to get drunk and screamy. At this point in the game, you can't control the outcome. You can only trust that you did the best you could and that everything is going to play out as it should. Clare Adama advises, "There are certain images you get in your head of how you want the day to go, how you hope people will react and so on—hold these lightly and don't try to force them to happen. If you get so caught up in a particular part of the wedding happening a certain way, you will be disappointed and often miss out on how brilliant and creative the reality is." You are pulling your wedding dress out of the closet. Your wedding is happening. It's time to let go of how you wish things were and instead tune in to how they are.

The No-Stress Deadline

Kimberly Greene, whose wedding came a year after her legal marriage, found that "for me, a non-procrastinator who has to have things done before she can relax, it was super helpful to have a no-more-stress deadline. Mine was two days before the wedding—after that, if something wasn't done, it wasn't getting done. And I honestly didn't care. It wasn't that kind of I-don't-care-on-the-outside-but-I'm-stressing-out-on-the-inside. I honestly just gave it up to Jesus. I mean, WWJD anyway? He wouldn't stress about anyone handing out some program fans, I'll bet you that much." Once your wedding day arrives, the program fans might not get passed out, but you're going to get married. So start paying attention to that.

Embrace Imperfection

Theory: On one of the most symbolically important days of your life, you are going to throw a high-stress, high-stakes party with a lot of moving pieces; all of your family is going to get together under one roof with a lot of booze and a lot of emotion; you're going to make an important, weighty lifetime commitment; and nothing is going to go wrong.

Practice: Things are going to go wrong.

There is a whole wedding marketing machine set up to sell you the perfect wedding, but the reality is, things are going to go wrong on your wedding day. That's fine. It's great, even. It's the imperfections that make the day yours. You may deal with a sound system that doesn't show up, or a wedding dress that rips at the altar, or a venue that can't seem to get anything right, or a friend who does something hurtful. Imperfection is human and inevitable. So go into your wedding day expecting small missteps, and do your best to embrace them when they come your way. Crystal Germond, who threw a smallish backyard wedding, learned, "Things weren't perfect by any means, but as my friend kept reminding me, beauty comes from imperfection. She literally kept telling me this every time I momentarily worried about food being cold or people not having fun or even flags getting twisted. She was so right." One of the gifts of your wedding day is the fact that you can choose, over and over again, in each moment, how you react to the things that go wrong. You can choose to allow the bigness of your commitment to take a front seat to the disappointments. "Perfect weddings don't exist," Anna Shapiro said. "Brides who say their weddings were perfect are women who made the conscious decision not to give a shit." So choose to let go, and choose to focus on the love filling the room. That is what you will remember in twenty years.

The Day Itself: Staying Present for the Whole Imperfect Thing

I'm not going to lie to you and say that being fully present on your wedding day is easy, but it is important. The key to fully experiencing your wedding day is surrender. The day is not going to be everything you hoped it would be; it's going to be more than that. Sometimes that's a good thing, and sometimes that's a hard thing. Because here is the honest truth:

Your wedding day might not feel like you expect it to feel.

After you read tons of wedding magazines and zillions of wedding blogs, it's hard not to have an idea of how your wedding day will feel. The thing is, that idea might be dead wrong. Anna Shapiro told me, "I thought I had a pretty good grip on how I would feel on the day of. I was wrong, and it is awesome that I was wrong. That is the beauty of it: the intense wave of emotions that swept over me, the desire to hug every single person that I'd ever met; I couldn't have foreseen it and I just needed to, well, feel it. We can predict all sorts of things, like the mood we will set with our music and decor, but we cannot predict what it will feel like in that very moment, and we should embrace that."

Popular wedding culture has taught us to focus on our dress, decorations, and details. We've all spent a lot of time planning how our wedding will look, and as a result we hope our wedding day is going to feel pretty and chic. The problem with this plan is that pretty and chic aren't emotions.

Trouble!

As my husband warned me before the wedding, it's really important to differentiate between how wedding pictures look and how your wedding day will feel. Our wedding pictures look dreamy and beautiful, and for that I'm grateful. Our wedding ceremony, on the other hand, felt intense, but not necessarily happy. And that was okay. There was plenty of time for joy at the party and in the weeks of bliss to come.

On the day itself, do everything you can to resist classifying your wedding-day emotions as right or wrong. Maybe like me, your life will change hard and fast, in a moment of gritty intensity. Maybe you'll ride a wave of joy, but at the end just feel like you threw an awesome party, nothing life-changing. Maybe you'll feel so overwhelmed that you'll weep for hours. Maybe it will be something totally different and even more unexpected. Whatever you feel, let yourself experience it. It may not be at all what you expected, and that may be a blessing.

Seeing Your Loved Ones: That Is Why You Are All Here

There is one profoundly good reason that you went through all the trouble it takes to plan a wedding: it gives you the chance to celebrate with your loved ones. The people who showed up to support you? Those are the right people. Crystal Germond described the end of her wedding this way: "Once night fell, we huddled around the bonfire and only went in the tent to get leftover food and pie. As the fire died, we threw our paper plates and wooden forks and decorations I'd spent so long cutting out with an X-Acto knife straight into the flames to keep us warm and together for just a little longer." The pretty parts of wedding planning are fun, but it all comes down to having the people you love in the same place, sharing the same moment. Luis Ramirez, who married his husband at Disneyland, told me, "A group of so many people important to us will probably not gather again until the last party that ever gets thrown for any-body, but we won't remember that one. That is the magic of a wedding." So breathe it in. This moment will stay with you for a long time to come and may end up bolstering you in ways you never could expect.

The Great Thing About Weddings Is You Can't Ruin Them

If there is one thing you take away from this chapter, let it be that it is really, really hard to ruin a wedding. Little things may go wrong, but you can choose to not let it matter. Susie Morrell learned from her small, funky Las Vegas wedding "that it can't be done wrong. It won't be perfect. You won't notice the chairs. Or the frozen margarita machine you paid for but never got. And you won't regret not doing something else. At least, we don't. When it comes down to it, none of that matters. You won't even care if your rings go missing." Fundamentally, you're there to get married. This is a huge and wonderful thing. It frees you from caring about frozen margarita machines, missing rings, and that detailed timeline you wrote, and allows you to just focus on the joy.

Beyond that, big things may go wrong. Emily Sterne Schebesta, who married in Boston, had her outdoor wedding completely rained out, which turned out to be a blessing in disguise. She said, "I really think the rain bonded us all together in a way that wouldn't have happened otherwise. Instead of the outdoor location we had intended for our ceremony, we were married in our reception tent, with the chairs arranged so that everyone was in a big circle around us." The key is rolling with what happens, letting go of your dreams for the day, and appreciating the reality of the moment.

It's possible that what seems like the biggest thing of all might go wrong: you won't love your wedding. Maybe you'll have fun, but it won't be the life-changing moment you expected. That's fine, too. "If you don't recognize a specific magical moment on your wedding day, it is okay. You have not failed," said Brooke Petermann, who married in Lincoln, Nebraska. "Maybe your entire day will be so subtly full of love that you just have to wait a few weeks or months for all of that goodness to accumulate in your postwedding brain." Or maybe you flat-out hated your wedding planning process, or something happened on your wedding day that left you in a puddle of tears. Though you might need to mourn the wedding you wish you'd had, you still get to move on with married life, where hopefully each day keeps getting better. Nicole Lozano, who had a handcrafted wedding bash in Texas, put it this way: "Did I love my wedding? No. I don't think the stress that I experienced was worth it. Was it a great party? Oh yeah! Am I glad I got married? Hell yes. The other side rocks." And that is why you can't ruin a wedding. If you're marrying a partner who makes you deeply happy, the wedding just becomes the party to kick off the rest of your life.

Planning a wedding is such a giddy mix of beautiful things combined with a serious dose of pain in the ass, so it's easy to get focused on This One Day We Spent So Much Time and Money Planning. But that day is not the point. Your marriage is the point. So as your wedding day approaches, remember that this too shall pass. And what you'll be left with is your marriage, which is infinitely more beautiful than the most stunning wedding dress in the world.

My wedding day was one of the great joys of my life. But the happiest day of my life? That was probably a lazy honeymoon day with my husband, drinking whiskey and looking at castles. Or maybe it was just any old lazy Sunday, reading the *New York Times*, lounging around the house . . . and, oh yeah, not planning a wedding.

THE PRACTICAL BRIDE REMEMBERS . . .

- Expect imperfection. The things that go wrong are what make the day yours.
- Well-laid plans allow you to have a laid-back wedding day, so do your planning homework.
- Remember to ask for help. You can't plan or execute a wedding alone, nor should you have to.
- Create a detailed day-of spreadsheet that outlines who is doing what and when on your wedding day.
- Hand over this spreadsheet, along with the rest of your planning, to a wedding stage manager (paid or unpaid) the day before your wedding.
- Create a timeline for the wedding day. Guests should feel like they are being guided from one activity to the next.
- Consider appointing a few emotional bodyguards, whose job it is to keep all stress and craziness away from you.
- Remember: weddings are stressful. If you find yourself wanting to kill someone, that's normal. Allow yourself to let it go and walk away.
- Set a no-stress deadline where you say, "f*ck it," and move from the planning to the doing.
- You get to choose how to react when things go wrong. Choose to let them go.
- Your wedding day may not feel how you expected it to feel. Try to embrace that as a blessing.
- The great thing about weddings is that you can't ruin them . . . because they always, always lead to marriages.

10

IT ACTUALLY
WASN'T THE BEST DAY
OF YOUR WHOLE LIFE

The End, and the Beginning

Finally, after all that planning, the wedding ends. Maybe your wedding felt like it went by in a flash, or maybe it felt like it stretched out for an eternity. But at some point it was over, and that's how it should be. Anyone who tells you that the wedding is the end has it wrong. The wedding is the beginning of your marriage. Megan Dunn described her reception as feeling like a "lovely afterglow" to the meaningful commitment made at the ceremony. Our weddings are about promising to spend the rest of our lives together. The party is an afterglow of that promise and the start of everything else.

Postwedding Freedom

You hear a lot of talk about postwedding depression, and it exists. You've spent a huge amount of energy planning a party, you've surfed an emotional high, and at some point you're going to crash. For me, that crash came in a hotel room in London, jet-lagged out of my mind, when I started crying about how I never wanted to forget how the wedding felt. I was glad to be married, but part of me was sad to be moving away from the great joy that was our wedding. If part of your identity has, however momentarily, become wrapped up in being a bride, it's natural that letting go of that identity can be a little sad. Allow yourself time to mourn. The wedding is over; your life has changed; you are coming back to reality. Some crying is normal.

But there is a parallel phenomenon that no one ever talks about: postwedding freedom. Shortly after our wedding we were browsing in a bookstore, and I stumbled upon a wedding magazine. I looked at it, and I had this dull feeling in the pit of my stomach. Then suddenly I realized, "It's not my problem anymore!" And I felt terribly free. Because the truth is, on a gut level, I was glad our wedding was over. It was an absurdly joyous day and an amazing party. But it was exactly the right length, and when it was over I dashed out the door, giddy with the knowledge of what we'd just done. I was thrilled that our wedding had been so happy, but I was equally delighted that I never had to plan it again and that I had the adventure of married life ahead of me.

When people say that your wedding is the happiest day of your life, they have it a little wrong. If all goes well, your wedding may be the happiest day of your life *so far*. But the wedding marks the beginning of married life; it is the announcement of the start of something great.

A PRACTICAL WIFE SPEAKS

The Love That Just Keeps Growing

BY ANDREA EISENBERG

On our wedding day, after my father gave an uproarious speech, he pulled me aside and told me there was something else he wanted to say in his speech but he didn't think he could include it without being misunderstood. He told me that if there was one thing he was certain about, it was that on that day, our wedding day, the day we'd chosen to stand in front of our friends and family to pledge our love and commitment to each other, that day was the day we would love each other least for the rest of our marriage.

It took me a minute to puzzle that out, because I was bursting with love and joy that day. But once I understood what he meant, that we would love each other more tomorrow than today, and more the day after that, too, I told him I hoped that was true.

Josh and I have been dealing with some difficult truths lately, but we are unbelievably fortunate to have each other every day.

I think back on our wedding day; it was only a year and a half ago, but what my father said is absolutely true. Compared to the love I have for him now, what I felt on our wedding day pales in comparison. I can hardly imagine the love we will share after decades of our life together.

At the time, I'd thought our wedding day was the happiest day of my life, but I can't begin to describe the relief we felt the day after the wedding—when we were married and we never had to do anything like that again. We could just get back to life as we knew it.

For a long time when people asked me, "How's married life?" I always gave them my stock answer, "'bout the same," but after a while I began to realize that wasn't exactly true. Little things started seeping in. When we fought, for example, even at our most vitriolic, things never really felt desperate—I knew this fight wouldn't be the death knell of our relationship. We'd fight and then afterward we'd still be married.

We're a pretty boring couple, actually; we don't get out much. We like cooking, drinking wine, playing with the dogs, and gardening. We started looking at houses. I never thought I'd be such a cookie-cutter wife, but I wanted a house, and right around the

[continues]

time I turned thirty I started wanting a baby. Fortunately, so did Josh.

Something funny happened when we started trying to get pregnant. I noticed my body wasn't working right. I'd never really paid attention before, but now it seemed so obvious. I went to the doctor. The diagnosis? I am unable to have children. At first we were floored. We were devastated. We'd talked about adoption before we got married, but we talked about it the same way we'd talked about what to do if one of us got hit by a bus. Could it happen? Sure, but we'd never entertained the idea that it was a real possibility.

That is, until it was our only possibility.

We took the time to grieve. To be honest, we're still grieving. I felt both betrayed and a betrayer—betrayed by my body and a betrayer to my husband, to our plan. On my worst day, I offered to walk away, to leave my husband so he could find a new wife, one who could give him the family he deserved. The look on his face told me he would never even consider it.

It was that day that I really understood our marriage.

Despite our insistence to leave all of that in sickness and in health, in good times and in bad, and in joy as well as in sorrow stuff out of our vows, it was another one of those things that crept in unnoticed.

I don't have a heartwarming end to this story yet. We are still on our journey, still suffering and still laughing together. But I feel like the tide has turned, and I think we will have our happy ending yet.

Even if it doesn't look like what we were expecting.

The Honeymoon: Time to Absorb the Inexplicable

The honeymoon is often marketed as the ultimate lavish escape: a time where you should spare no expense to have the perfect vacation. Because of that, if you're strapped for cash to spend on your wedding or have limited vacation time, it seems obvious that you should cut the honeymoon and jump right back into life after the wedding. I'd advise against that.

For most of us, our wedding ends up being an intense emotional experience. Sometimes everything goes well and you are over the moon. Sometimes you had to face up to difficult emotional truths, and you are exhausted. But after going through all that together, chances are good that you're going to need some time off, just the two of you, to process what just happened.

And the truth is, you only get one chance to have the emotional bonding experience that is the postwedding honeymoon (though you'll have many chances to take fabulous vacations). The honeymoon allows you to bliss out and to try to absorb the magnitude of what you've just done together. Your wedding is a major life event, even if it's not the most important day of your life. Maybe you feel like it changes you in some intangible way; maybe your relationship feels exactly the same. But you will be tired, you will have the words "husband" or "wife" to get used to, new rings to stare at, and a party to talk over. So whether you jet off on an exotic adventure or just take four days in your apartment with an unplugged phone, take some time off, together. Think about what just happened. Savor being a brand-new family. Ponder the adventures ahead of you. Enjoy being married. And for goodness' sake, take a few naps.

Wishing You Love That Keeps on Growing

Wedding planning is a trial by fire. It forces you to grapple with the tough issues: faith, family, friendship. It usually leads to some arguments, or at least some thoughtful discussions. And no matter what, wedding planning forces you to make choices. Hopefully, this book has helped encourage you to say yes to things that are meaningful to you and a calm but firm no to things that are wrong for you. Hopefully, you've fought through the hard parts and emerged on the other side with a hard-won sense of what matters to you and what doesn't. Think of this as practice.

Married life, and the family that the two of you just made together, does not have to look any one way. Married life is what you create; it's about what you dream up together. Sara Hilliard Garratt said that after she and her husband pulled off a wedding that felt like an uncompromising reflection of who they were, they thought, "Together, we could do anything we set our minds to." And so they did. After a lot of discussion about the life they wanted to live, and the family they wanted to grow into, they decided to embark on the wildest plan they could think of: sailing across the Pacific and exploring the Pacific Rim. And then, crazily enough, they did it.

For most us, creating a family life won't look quite that extreme, but hopefully it will look quietly brave. Maybe you'll decide to travel the world together; maybe one of you will start your own business, or go to grad school. Maybe you'll have kids young, or resist pressure and wait until you feel ready, or never have kids at all. Maybe you'll move to a farm, or stick with your tiny city apartment, or fully embrace the suburbs. But hopefully you'll make thoughtful choices with great grace, just like you did during wedding planning.

When marriage goes right, it allows us to be stronger people together than we would be apart. Shortly after her marriage, Catherine Sly said, "Our dear friend stood up at our wedding and confidently proclaimed, 'Marriage makes you free.' And I have no idea how he knew it, but he was right." Marriage allows us to support our partners to become the people they were meant to be. To empower them to pursue their dreams, and to live bravely and honestly. It allows us to live bravely and honestly ourselves. Marriage gives us the strength to continue to say yes to what is right for us. It gives us a foundation on which to build and the strength to dream big dreams.

My wish for you is not just a happy wedding. My real wish is that married life makes you free, that being a family allows you to be your bravest self. My dream is that the foundation of your marriage allows you to offer support to your community in the same way that your loved ones offered you support on your wedding day. I hope that on most days, you remember how lucky you are to be married to your partner. Mostly I hope that you have many long and happy years supporting and loving each other. If that happens, your wedding was just a whisper of the magic that is to come. I can't wait to see what you create.

THE PRACTICAL WIFE REMEMBERS . . .

- After the wedding, you may experience an emotional crash. But you may also experience a rush of postwedding freedom. You never have to plan this thing again, and you have your whole married lives ahead of you.

- Consider taking a honeymoon after the wedding, even if you just go a few miles outside of town. Or stay home, unplug your phones, and tell everyone you've left. After going through such a huge life experience together, you and your partner will probably need some time to bliss out, adjust, and take naps.

- Wedding planning forced you to make choices that were right for you, even when that was hard. Allow this to carry over to your married life, as you make choices that shape your new family.

- Marriage makes us free. Free to support our partners, free to become who we were meant to be. Let marriage allow you to create a life that's right for you. Here's wishing you many happy and brave years!

MEET
TEAM PRACTICAL

The many people who have shared their stories and comments on APracticalWedding.com over the years have helped to shape my sense of what weddings and marriages can be. Here are the handful of those smart women and men I quoted in this book.

Clare Adama lives in Scotland, where she has spent far too much time studying theology and is now putting this into practice by supporting faith groups and engaging in anti-poverty community transformation work. She is happiest as a geek, a friend, a wife, a baker, and an APW fan.

Anna Alter is a children's book author and illustrator living in western Massachusetts with her husband, daughter, and two cats. She got married in the summer of 2009 under a maple tree in the Berkshires. You can find out more about her work and her crafty wedding at her blog, Painting Bunnies: annaalter.blog spot.com.

Harrison Caudill is a no-nonsense software engineer married to a dreamy geneticist (Elizabeth). He survived his wedding by remembering to breathe and his marriage by remembering to laugh. See his out-of-date website if you are curious: hyper sphere.org.

Lauren Davis Wojtkun lives with her husband, Jeff Davis, and their cat, Foxxy, in Arlington, Massachusetts, where she loves the summers and hates the winters. She writes about marriage, home ownership, turning thirty-something, and striving for more out of life over at her blog, Suburbalicious Living (suburb aliciousliving.blogspot.com).

Lisa M. G. Dennis (www.missgiggles.com) has taught elementary school and college, gotten through graduate school once and is doing it again, run marathons, lived abroad, and tried belly dancing. However, family and marriage have been her greatest adventures. She looks forward to the rest of her exciting life, now to be shared with her best friend.

Sara Downey is a writer and social media strategist living in Denver. A former derby girl with the Denver Roller Dolls, Sara now maintains her agility by changing her newborn son's diapers in under sixty seconds while dodging the inevitable surprise pee stream. You can follow her adventures at www.meanest look.com.

Caitlin Driscoll Cannon lives in New York City and works at trying to save the world (or at least a small piece of it) for a national environmental organization. After submitting her Wedding Graduate post to A Practical Wedding and finding support from Meg's readers, she felt brave enough to start writing on her own about loss, marriage, and moving on at onwardfulltilt.blog spot.com.

Kirsten Duke is a twenty-five-year-old public health policy analyst who lives in Ottawa, Ontario, Canada, with her husband, Aaron, and their pug/Boston terrier mix, Lucy. Kirsten is also a food blogger, whose thoughts on food and restaurants in Ottawa can be found at poptartsandbacon.blogspot.com.

Megan Dunn is a midwife in Olympia, Washington. For her, the highlight of three days of wedding festivities that included a taco truck picnic, 5k fun run, homemade pies, home-brewed beer, contra dancing, and sparklers was the Quaker wedding ceremony, during which all those present had a chance to share their thoughts, blessings, memories, and wisdom.

Kimberly Eclipse is a counselor and the creator of ABrave Life.com, where she writes about how to design a balanced, beautiful, and ballsy life for oneself. She lives in New York with her husband and their two cats, all three of whom she describes as being "cute, hairy, and fabulous roommates."

Michelle Edgemont is a designer who lives in Brooklyn with her musician husband, Adam. Her wedding, although stressful to plan, turned out to be the most fun she has ever had in one day. She likes spending time with her family, big bowls of candy, and making crafts. You can find her at www.Michelle Edgemont.com.

Andrea Eisenberg lives in Chicago with her handsome and witty husband, Josh, two funny dogs, two crazy cats, and (surprise!) a sweet baby boy named Henry. She is an engineer by trade but prefers spending her time knitting, cooking, gardening, and drinking hoppy beers in the sun. Her online home is www.themaidenmetallurgist.com.

Maddie Eisenhart is a somewhat newly married lady living in Connecticut with her husband, Michael, and their really, really, really big dog, Juno. Sometimes she puts headphones on and listens to Styx full blast while pretending to do housework.

Desaray Evans is a social worker living in Asheville, North Carolina. Eighteen months after the wedding, Desaray's wife fell in love with someone else and ended the marriage. Desaray now fills up her middle by thinking about beginnings and endings. She can be found embarking upon single motherhood, fostering abandoned puppies, being a hospice volunteer, and collecting stories about love, loss, and food at foodfuneral.wordpress.com.

Having fallen in love with Mr. Darcy by the age of ten, it came as no surprise to many that **Marchelle Farrell** should meet her own complex Englishman, while transplanted from her tropical Trinidadian home to first study medicine, then work unsociable hours in England. Dear reader, she married him.

Steffany Farros is from the San Francisco Bay area. She's been known to venture into the wild world of DIY foodstuffs and return with fresh cheese and loaves of bread. When she is not in the kitchen she is probably reading or playing a board game with her insatiable game-designer husband. She writes at www.dinnerlove.com.

Jamie Fergerson and **Max Green** live in queerly wedded bliss in the Deep South. They fill their free time working for social justice, reading, writing, and loving their two bossy dogs and three sneaky cats. Jamie and Max are grateful to have found each other and to be a part of a beloved community.

Jessica Flaherty resides in Maine with her husband, Stewart, and their beagle, Dash. Jessica practices family and criminal law, and Stewart is a soccer coach at a local college. They view their marriage, much like their wedding, as a work in progress!

Cara Forbes-Stenning lives in Glasgow with her husband, twin baby girls, and rabbit. She writes at www.peoniesandpolaroids .com, and photographs weddings with her husband for their business, www.lillianandleonard.com. She likes pancakes, stripes, and big dogs. She dislikes team sports, macaroons, weak coffee, and photos of French girls on bicycles.

Crystal Germond, "The Esthete," is a native of Woodstock, New York. A "full-time idealist," Crystal works toward social justice and in her spare time pursues passion-filled hobbies like makeup artistry and yoga. She lives in Boston with her husband, Ananth, and two dogs ("the girls"). Marvel with her at theesthete.tumblr.com or @TheEsthete on Twitter.

Kimberly Greene is a writer working in the publishing industry. When she doesn't have her nose in a book, she's either knitting, watching *House Hunters*, or plotting the next escape to one of her must-get-to travel destinations. She lives with her husband and their cat in Toronto, Canada. Find her at Someone Seeking Up: eclpse.livejournal.com.

Emily Gutman lives with her husband in Oakland, California. She is the owner of Emily Takes Photos (www.emilytakes photos.com) and a longtime member of the APW community. In her free time, she loves to cook, craft, and lindy hop. Emily also wants to teach middle school when she grows up.

Kristiina Hackel is a professor of film, television, and media studies at California State University, Los Angeles. An award-winning filmmaker, screenwriter, and sometime blogger, she muses about weddings at www.theimaginarywedding.com.

Brandi Hassouna can be found either with her nose in a nursing textbook or playing in the kitchen. She and her husband try to live as car free as they can in LA. Their first child will also be sleeping in a closet. Wish them luck.

Kayce Hazelgrove is a web developer by day who started her blog Shiny Pretty Bits (shinyprettybits.com) as a means to navigate the confusing waters of wedding planning for a thirty-something with a nontraditional family. These days she can be found blogging about her food adventures at Foodie Was Here (foodiewashere.com).

Caitlin Helms and her husband, Kyle, were married in a small ceremony at her family's cabin in northern Minnesota. Immediately following their honeymoon, they moved to Cincinnati, Ohio, where she currently works as a nurse while he completes a PhD. They have added a dog named Olive to their new family. www.webecomeus.wordpress.com.

Sara Hilliard Garratt and her new husband, Stof, left their home and a budding legal career in Cape Town, South Africa, to explore the Pacific and their marriage via sail, road, and rail in 2011 and 2012. She writes about life and their voyage at www.stofnsara.com.

Sharon Hsu got married on a Saturday and moved across the country the following Wednesday for graduate school. The process wasn't nearly as terrifying as it sounds, since her favorite person went with her. She now lives in the San Francisco Bay area with her husband and an overwhelming number of books.

Christen Karle Muir's geographic background is much like her personality—midwestern values, East Coast work ethic, and a

West Coast outlook. Christen is a professional theatre actor performing throughout San Francisco. Additionally, she works as a personal assistant, floral designer, voiceover artist, and office manager. When not scrabbling to make a living, Christen enjoys photography, holistic nutrition, making stuff, and getting dirt between her toes. She lives with her husband and her son, Silas, in San Francisco.

Nicole Kazee is a former professor and forever policy wonk. She's a triathlete, yogi, and golfer who suspects she's solar powered. She's also a North Carolinian who finds herself transplanted in Chicago (by way of New York, by way of Connecticut, by way of Washington, D.C., by way of Japan). Happily married, natch.

Fred Keene (Meg's dad) teaches math. He is a son of a marine, and went to college at MIT and graduate school at "Berkeley in the '60s." He got married in Grace Cathedral in San Francisco to Meg's mom, Hannah. They have two cool daughters, Meg and Sarah. Fred likes having daughters.

Hannah Keene (Meg's mom) is a fifth-grade teacher. She got married to Meg's dad because there was nothing he didn't know something about, and because he made her laugh. (He still does.) They have the two best grown daughters in the world.

Megan Kongaika has a master of science degree in public relations from Montana State University, Billings. She lives and works in Montana with her husband, who continues to pleasantly surprise her on a daily basis. She can be found at www.meganithappen.blogspot.com.

Marie-Ève Laforte lives in Montreal with her husband and two young children. After completing her master's degree in literature in Europe, she returned to Quebec and became a technical writer, journalist, freelancer, and avid blogger (marie-eve laforte.blogspot.com). After years of doing wedding flowers for everyone around her, she decided to pursue this passion further.

Ashley and Zach LaMotte live in the Chicago suburbs with their fur babies, Max the cat and Rigby the Boston terrier. During the day, Ashley works at a national nonprofit and Zach tunes and teaches piano. Outside work, they can be found going to concerts, playing with Rigby, crafting, and blogging at www.squirreled-away.com.

Dana LaRue is editor-in-chief of her award-winning blog, the Broke-Ass Bride (thebrokeassbride.com), empowering couples to use creativity as currency to craft bad-ass weddings without breaking the bank. Basically, if Oprah and Suze Orman had a baby, and Carrie Bradshaw and Mary Poppins had a baby . . . and their babies had a baby? Yeah, she'd be that baby.

Nicole Lozano, originally from Texas, is a reader, writer, pseudo-gardener, baker, and record-collecting student working on her PhD in the Midwest. She married her college sweetheart in a big wedding in 2009, even though she wanted to elope.

Anna and Mike Mahony live in a cozy house next to a creek in Northern California. If they won the lottery, they would divide their time between speed Scrabble, learning to play new instruments passably well, and taking naps in the backyard.

Stephanie Marienau Turpin works in international development and peace-building. She enjoys writing, exploring new places, and serving the church. She and her husband, John, were married in June 2010 in Washington, D.C.

Alyssa Mooney received a bachelor of arts in theatre and a minor in gender studies from Stephen F. Austin State University. She lives in Dallas, Texas, with her adorably redneck husband and Maggie the Wonder Dog. Alyssa is columns editor on A Practical Wedding and can also be found at KindofaMess.com.

Liz Moorhead lives in Philly with a house full of men—her husband, Joshua, her son, Josh Jr., and Salvador the cat. She teaches high school English and, when not arbitrating the dramatic entanglements of teenagers, sells hand-painted notecards through her shop, Betsy Ann Paper. Visit Liz's blog at www .happysighs.com.

Susie Morrell is an American writer living in Ireland. She married her Irish sweetheart in Las Vegas in October 2009. A Massachusetts native, Susie loves road trips, baseball, and her husband's cooking. She lives in Dublin, Ireland, with husband Neil and their dog, Sausage.

Britta Nielsen lives in Seattle with her husband, Adam, and their cat, Princess Isabella. They spend their weekends either relaxing, playing house, or participating in rally motorsports events in the woods. You can find her at www.brittanielsen .com.

Karen Palmer will marry her college sweetheart in an intimate ceremony in Burlington, Vermont, in September 2012. She lives in Chicago with her fiancé and their two dogs, and works as a nonprofit fundraiser, where event planning takes up approximately 40 percent of her time.

Katie Pegher is a bride-to-be from Pittsburgh who is finally starting to embrace the idea of being a "bride," though she will absolutely refuse to allow anyone to take a photo of her gazing wistfully out a window.

Shana and Morgan Pellitteri spent three years in Los Angeles learning weird things about life and love before returning east to share them. They grew up in the Catskill Mountains, where echoes of their wedding-day laughter still ring from the hills at sunset. Listen . . .

Brooke Petermann had a practical wedding that was pretty and fabulous and now has a marriage that is fabulous, although it is not always pretty. Brooke is the creative force behind www.graceandlightstudio.com. She loves happy and modern design and is particularly passionate about modern cross-stitching.

Anna Plumb lives in Portland, Oregon, with her husband and two ridiculous cats. During the day, she gets paid to tell people how to be better at their jobs. At night, she gleefully eats her husband's cooking and tries not to complain about doing the dishes.

Luis Ramirez lives in Long Beach, California, with his husband, Michael, and two cats with obvious entitlement issues. The husbands were wed during the short window of time it was legal for them to do so in California, and they are waiting for the federal government to get its head out of its ass.

Brianne Sanchez is a recovering journalist who lives in (surprisingly awesome) Des Moines, Iowa, with her husband, Joe, and their fox-dog, Wilbur. She currently blogs at BSintheMidwest

.com but tries not to spend all her time in front of the computer when there are adventures to be had.

A resident of Oregon via Missouri via Alaska, **Lynn Schell** fills her life utilizing her innate talent for assessment and analysis to create entirely new systems whose primary aim is to expand learning, to create an entirely new and larger vision for all. She's too often a perfectionist but thrives on taking big risks.

Matthew Seymour and **Becky Leach-Seymour** live in Columbus, Ohio. When they aren't working, Becky in nonprofit fundraising and Matt in marketing and sales, they enjoy traveling and working on their house. More about their wedding, the planning process, and DIY projects they have tackled can be found at Becky's blog, bridezillatobebecky.blogspot.com.

Kathleen Shannon is an art director turned free-spirited freelance designer and an on-her-way-to-being-sort-of-a-big-deal blogger with a style perspective that pervades everything from her clothes, to her home, to her food. Find her at www.jeremy andkathleen.blogspot.com.

Anna Shapiro is a neurotic academic whose wedding planning experience was harrowing; whose actual wedding was imperfect and perfect at the same time; and whose postnuptial life is liberating. She really thinks you should go on a honeymoon.

Marisa-Andrea Moore Shelby is an attorney and writer from California. She is an admitted hopeless romantic and tries to do something courageous and outside of her comfort zone each day. She has been married for three wonderful years to a man who makes her roll on the floor with laughter constantly.

Catherine Sly is a twenty-seven-year-old married Brit with one daughter. A linguistics graduate, she is currently working for herself from home as a registered child minder while working toward becoming a qualified counselor. In her spare time she likes to write (at projectsubrosa.com), take photos and spend time with her family.

Christine and Curtis Smith are in their late thirties and live in southeastern Massachusetts along with their three babies (i.e., cats). They had a two-year engagement so they could pay off their credit card debt, convert their house from oil to gas, and pay cash for all things wedding related. Practical indeed!

Jen Smith is a perfectionistic control freak and engineer. She loves dogs whose heads are hanging out the windows of cars, children who have clearly dressed themselves, the color purple, both eating and baking pie, and taking everything out of kitchen cabinets, cleaning them out, and putting everything back inside.

Emily Sterne Schebesta is a wedding photographer living in Cambridge, Massachusetts, with her husband, son, and high-maintenance cat. Her wedding in 2009 was the rainiest, muddiest, most love-filled day she can remember. It brings her great joy to capture in photographs the love-filled (not always rainy) wedding days of other nice people. You can find her at emilysterne.com.

Emma Straub is a writer. She and her husband, graphic designer Michael Fusco, live in Brooklyn, and three years later are still really glad they had a small wedding. www.mplusedesign.com.

Emily Threlkeld attended Edgar Allen Poe Elementary School, Sidney Lanier Middle School, and a high school that was not named after a writer, but by that point it was too late. She recently earned a BFA in student loan accumulation with a minor in poetry. You can find her at www.threlkelded.net.

Morgan Turigan lives with her husband, David, in Calgary, Alberta. She's living her childhood dream of working in a shiny office tower and spending all of her disposable income on travel and other fun things. She enjoys oil painting, reading, planning the next vacation, and restoring midcentury furniture.

Lindsay Whitfield is a proud mum, loving wife, and energetic kindergarten teacher. Her interests include antique furniture, community organizing, Douglas Coupland, dirndls, and the monarchy. She does not care for jazz, the flavor "chocolate mint," or long flights featuring crying infants. She bakes the best lemon squares in the universe.

Molly Wiedel Till got married to a seriously amazing guy. They had an amazing time planning their wedding and an amazing time at their wedding. Now, they're starting the hard work of creating an amazing baby family. Molly is seriously thankful to have A Practical Wedding to keep her and her guy sane. And amazing.

Cara Winter lives in Brooklyn, New York, with her husband, Jeff Kirsch. For business, she investigates engineering failures of the built world. For pleasure, she investigates the Brooklyn dining scene, Hudson Valley bed-and-breakfasts, vintage Americana, and a new hobby every few months. She tweets @cara herself.

FIND MORE RESOURCES ON
APRACTICALWEDDING.COM

I've tried to pack this book as full of ideas as possible, but somehow it seems that there is always a little more to say about weddings, always another question to answer. Luckily, APractical Wedding.com is updated every day with resources for planning a sane wedding and an adventurous married life. Here is a list of resources you can find on the site:

Online wedding resources: I maintain a list of the best (and sanest) online wedding resources I can find. Web resources come and go, so check the site for an up-to-date list.

How-to: If you're looking to take on a DIY project not covered in Chapter 6, chances are there is a tutorial on how to do it as simply as possible on APW.

Downloadable spreadsheets: If the idea of creating a Day-Of Spreadsheet from scratch makes you feel bonkers, you're in luck. We've created spreadsheets you can download, fill in, and go.

A vendor and venue directory: When you're looking for products and services for your wedding, the trick is finding people you like and trust. On APW we've created a list of vendors who have signed our sanity pledge, along with a list of venues that readers loved.

Real weddings: Each chapter in the book opened with a first-person story of a wedding day, and APW is chock-full of these stories, called "Wedding Graduates." Couples share the story of what they learned and what they'd tell their planning self if they could go back in time.

Reclaiming Wife: A wedding is an amazing celebration of commitment and a huge party. But what's really important is what comes next—married life. APW has a whole section of the site dedicated to navigating married life with grit and grace.

SELECTED SOURCES

I depended on the following books while writing, many of which I suggest readers pick up for further information, or just delightful hours of reading.

The bulk of my research on the history of weddings in America came from the enthralling *All Dressed in White: The Irresistible Rise of the American Wedding* by Carol McD. Wallace (Penguin Books, 2004). I also used *Brides, Inc.: American Weddings and the Business of Tradition* by Vicki Howard (University of Pennsylvania Press, 2006), which offers an excellent exploration of the entwined nature of consumerism and American wedding tradition. I found information on the relatively new—and arguably faux—tradition of the unity candle in *One Perfect Day: The Selling of the American Wedding* by Rebecca Mead (Penguin Press, 2007). Beyond that, *One Perfect Day* helped guide my own wedding planning and wedding thinking, and it is a page-turning must-read for anyone headed down the aisle.

My perspective on all things wedding, and particularly wedding etiquette, has been unalterably shaped by the brilliant Judith Martin, whose Miss Manners books I have been reading since I was tall enough to drag them off the shelf (I must note that my parents, seemingly intentionally, placed them on very low shelves). In writing this book, I have particularly depended on *Miss Manners' Guide to Excruciatingly Correct Behavior* (W. W. Norton & Company, 2005) and *Miss Manners' Guide to a Surprisingly Dignified Wedding* (W. W. Norton & Company, 2010), cowritten with Jacobina Martin. If you haven't already read these, please do.

The way I approach wedding ceremonies was certainly influenced by the now classic *The New Jewish Wedding* by Anita Diamant (Fireside, 1985). Also, *Celebrating Interfaith Marriages: Creating your Jewish/Christian Ceremony* by Rabbi Devon A. Lerner (Henry Holt and Company, 1999) is the single best liturgical resource I've found for thinking about constructing a wedding service.

For more information on how the brain responds to choice, I recommend *The Paradox of Choice: Why More Is Less* by Barry Schwartz (HarperCollins, 2004). This book helped me make better decisions for our own wedding, and informed what I wrote about planning here.

In this book I've also quoted *Emma* by Jane Austen (1816; Bantam Dell, 2004); *Pitching My Tent* by Anita Diamant (Scribner, 2003); and *A Jew Today* by Elie Wiesel (Vintage Books, 1979).

And finally, this book, and APracticalWedding.com, would not have been possible without *Offbeat Bride: Creative Alternatives for Independent Brides* by Ariel Meadow Stallings (Seal Press, 2010) and her eponymous website, OffbeatBride.com. Ariel blazed the trail for progressive, no-nonsense wedding planning. For that I am profoundly grateful, both personally and professionally.

ACKNOWLEDGMENTS

First, thanks must be given to David's and my family, for their love and support. In particular, I am grateful to my parents, Hannah and Fred Keene, for unquestioningly believing that I will accomplish anything I set my mind to, which is of course a bit of a self-fulfilling prophecy. Also many thanks to my grandmother Jane Crittenden, who was always just as excited about our marriage as she was about our wedding, and who reminded me that all of this could be done sensibly, as it had been for generations.

Further thanks go to my agent, Maura Teitelbaum, for fiercely promoting the project, always having my back, and sharing my outrage at cake-cutting fees. And this book wouldn't be in your hands without my editor, Katie McHugh, who got the why of the book immediately.

I wouldn't have had the time to write this without the support of my excellent staff, both past and present: Lauren Dupuis-Perez, for organizing everything and working tirelessly; Alyssa Mooney, for always making me laugh and taking on more than she needed to; and Emily Gutman, for helping to manage the business side of things and sharing my love of profits.

A chapter of praise should be written about Kate Bolen, who beyond being an amazing friend and the very first reader of my blog, edited every word of this document, from dubious rough draft to more polished final draft. She offered encouragement, made me meet weekly deadlines, copy edited, and content edited. She stayed up late, bought me colored binder clips, and generally made it possible for someone who is dyslexic to become a published author without a single nervous breakdown.

My heart is full of gratitude for my ladies of the Internet, who have been there for me every day for the past four years. They told me it was okay to dream big, and supported me through all the ups and downs of bringing a book into the world, not to mention the ups and downs of living in the world. They fill up my life with the richness of color and the texture of dreams. Heartfelt thanks go to Amanda Bruns, Cate Sly, Cara Forbes-Stenning, Jamie Street, Lisa Carnochan, Marchelle Farrell, and Marie-Ève Laforte, not to mention many other women who love me through the Internet every single day.

Beyond that, it takes a village: I live in awe of the ladies who read APW and make the community thrive. I was honored to quote a handful of the smart women and men who shared their wedding stories on APW, but owe a debt of gratitude to many more Wedding Graduates. Team Practical and the APW community helped shape my philosophy on laid-back, no-nonsense weddings, in a way I can't possibly express on the page. This book wouldn't be the same without them.

I probably never would have learned to write with clarity and honesty without my high school English teachers, Cheryl and Harry Syphus. Not only did they teach me to write, but they were also responsible for finally getting my husband and me together after years of friendship laced with tremendously enjoyable enmity. Their insistence that David look me up in New York City turned a worthy opponent into a worthy opponent I would build a life with.

And finally, none of this would have been possible without David, who is truly a husband among husbands. He was the one who told me, while I was crying (again) during the early days of wedding planning, that I should start a blog and call it A Practical Wedding. He believed in the project every step of the way and insisted that I get an agent, write the proposal, do the work, and never give up. He makes me laugh, endlessly, and keeps me going, always. For all that, I am enormously grateful and profoundly devoted, and will forever be cheering him on.

INDEX